CALIFORNIA CRAZY

CALIFORNIA CRAZY

ALAN CARTNAL

BOSTON
HOUGHTON MIFFLIN COMPANY
1981

This book is published by special arrangement
with Eric Lasher and Maureen Lasher.

Portions of this book originally appeared, in slightly
different form, in *New West* magazine and *Penthouse*.

Copyright © 1981 by Alan Cartnal

All rights reserved. No part of this work may be reproduced
or transmitted in any form by any means, electronic or
mechanical, including photocopying and recording, or by
any information storage or retrieval system, without
permission in writing from the publisher.

Library of Congress Cataloging in Publication Data

Cartnal, Alan.
California crazy.

1. California — Social life and customs.
2. California — Popular culture. I. Title.
F866.2.C37   979.4'9053   80-27315
ISBN 0-395-28213-6

Printed in the United States of America

P 10 9 8 7 6 5 4 3 2 1

For my mother and father

ACKNOWLEDGMENTS

My warmest appreciation goes to Maureen and Eric Lasher, whose love and talent helped to shape this book; to my wonderful editor, Ellen Joseph, for her support and undying enthusiasm; and to Austin Olney, editor in chief at Houghton Mifflin Co., for his wisdom and impeccable taste.

In addition, I want to express my gratitude to my friends Joseph Loving, Charles Hallam, Sandra Becker, and Steve Piekarski for their support, laughter, and outrageousness. I love you.

CONTENTS

	Beverly Hills — The Introduction	1
1	Brentwood — The Women	3
2	The Religion	19
3	Boys Town — The Weekend	33
4	The Hustler	45
5	The Hostess	59
6	Boys Town — The Weekend	67
7	Bel Air — The Rock Star	75
8	The Restaurant	93
9	The Fad	105
10	Malibu — The Movie Star	117
11	Newport Beach — The Matron	133
12	Boys Town — The Weekend	147
13	The Dope Dealer	155
14	The Teen Idol	165
15	The Shopper	175
16	Boys Town — The Weekend	183
17	The Party	187

CALIFORNIA CRAZY

BEVERLY HILLS—THE INTRODUCTION

10 A.M., BEVERLY HILLS

CHER BONO ALLMAN is tooling down the main shopping thoroughfares of Beverly Hills. She is looking very strung out. There are people sort of fainting in the streets as the Queen of Chic makes her daily rounds shopping. Cher is dressed like an Indian princess today. Yesterday she wore a veil, a character from Scheherazade. The day before she appeared in a jogging outfit.

Suddenly there is a tremor of life. Her bone-thin knees begin to shake. Her expression resembles that of a housewife on "The Price is Right" who has just discovered that she has won the grand prize. Cher Bono Allman is very happy. Inside a VW parked at the side of the road she has spotted a dress. Not just any dress. But *the* dress that she needs tomorrow. She rushes over and pounds on the window. The driver, a woman in her twenties with sun-flecked brown hair, a California type who looks as if she probably does meditation exercises and eats wheat bran nonpreservative bread, is alarmed. For a minute she doesn't recognize that it is Cher, the Queen of Chic, who is pounding at her window. She takes a gun from her glove compartment. Cher doesn't care. She keeps pounding on the window and begins to scream: "I'VE GOT TO TALK TO YOU." Then the woman recognizes Cher and rolls down her window. Cher tells her to open the door. They are soon chatting like old friends in the VW while a crowd of people watches this whole scene with interest. Cher says, "Look, honey, I've got to buy that dress in your back seat. I've got to have it. See, I wanna have something special to show to Diana Ross today. I mean she's seen all the junk in the stores. But, this is something that would blow her mind." Cher gives the woman a check for $100. She takes the dress from the back seat. And she walks off into the sun-specked day, smiling the Cher smile.

1 BRENTWOOD-THE WOMEN

CAROLE WITH AN "E" was bored with making it with the Sparklett's man. She pretended she wasn't at home that morning when he buzzed the bell at the back door of her spacious country estate in one of the canyons bursting with beautiful homes in exclusive Brentwood. The Sparklett's man must have been very horny. For twenty minutes he pounded on the back door and yelled her name, like a lost child searching for its mother. But Carole had decided that the fun was over. This was it.

Six times, in every sex-manual position, in practically every room in the house, was enough. Carole *was* missing the scent of sandalwood and the aroma of grass which seeped into every crease of his green workingman's overalls. She didn't feel guilty, however. *That* was Victorian. The age of sex being dirty was over. She was much "too big" to be victimized by the Southern California deliverymen she seduced over and over again.

The last two sessions had been degrading. He had delivered the water bottles to the kitchen, walked without speaking to the living room, smoked a joint, undressed until he was nude, and demanded a blow job. He had not even asked her to undress. His manner had frightened her slightly and aroused her even more. He had been a football player at Palisades High. He did have the silkiest, smoothest skin on the most beautifully proportioned body Carole had ever beheld. But there would be others. Brentwood was a playground, and Carole's sexual desires equaled the size of her husband's fortune.

Something was wrong, of course. Something she couldn't put her finger on at that moment. It wasn't that Carole was a nymphomaniac. It was just that most days she had sex at least seven times, and sometimes she couldn't remember the names of her partners. Sex for Carole had become as casual as changing sheets.

As Carole combed her hair and dressed she reviewed the previous day's conquests. She had infidelity down to a science. She would dress her little girl and send her off to school. Take care of her husband's lust and douche.

Carole had made up her mind that she just wasn't going to participate in the sad and lonely routines of a wealthy Brentwood wife. Talking to the gardener all day about bougainvillea was not her idea of a good time. Exercise classes were classified as pitsville. Almost as deadly dull as dialing girlfriends and pleading with them to come over for lunch. Carole wanted the status symbols and labels she was expected to acquire to keep up with the Brentwood set. She would drink mineral water to appear cool. Take the tennis lessons and the jogging instruction. But Carole was secretly longing for the perfect sexual partner. What was the good of valet parking and drinking nothing but white wine and walking down Rodeo Drive and seeing ten people who were at her house the night before unless she could come up with a trick. Carole had made up her mind that promiscuity was where it was at.

Men were no problem in Brentwood. She knew exactly how to dress to give the impression of being the absolute quintessence of the California Dream. What perfume to wear. How to bring out that something extra in men when she undressed before them in the little white-picket-fence motels up on Sunset.

Something was missing, of course. She had spoken to most of the other women of her set about *it*. Had been jealous that in the other extramarital affairs the men treated women romantically and with concern. But, what the hell, she was bored. There were just so many shops. Just so many expensive cars. Just so many $500 negligees. Some women took up knitting and daytime TV. Carole took up sex.

Carole needed a quickie, in fact, before lunch that noon at Rainbow's End in Brentwood Village. So she rushed through her daily cellulite exercise routine in order to be out of the house by ten. Instead of driving the black Mercedes to Beverly Hills she headed in the opposite direction, toward the beach. She noticed a couple of roadside gardeners giving her the eye. But she wanted a Good Daddy type. Brentwood was crawling with them. Decent, upstanding executives with wives and kids who had come to California to make it happen and worked sixteen hours a day. They usually had business-expense lunches at restaurants that featured casual cuisine and overlooked the beach.

Carole knew a secluded spot where some of the lustful loners would park to take advantage of a brief moment, viewing the natural wonders of the Pacific. She looked damned good that day. Carole was always beautiful, but on a few days of the year she could look absolutely spectacular. This was one of those days. Her long, red hair gleamed like a model's in a beauty advertisement. Her lavender eyes filled with sparkle. Her amazingly youthful body captured fully by a frilly, plunging designer dress.

Carole popped a Valium. Thrilled to the billowing, surrealistic clouds forming in the west. Watched the tropical blue sea toss and turn and let the waves and the sun-drenched waters engulf her. Then she gracefully exited from the car and positioned herself seductively against the back end. She smoked a cigarette nonchalantly. It wasn't long before the construction crews nearby noticed.

One of them, not a decent daddy but a young, short-haired redneck type wearing an extra-large T-shirt bearing the inscription IRAN SUCKS and a cap with Chevrolet written on its front, approached. He sported a couple of tattoos on his arms. Carole threw down the cigarette and smiled.

"Do you wanna get laid?"

That was all Carole ever said.

═══════

What in the hell *was* the agenda today, anyway? Was the poolman coming? Jesus, the filter system was on the blink again. Was she supposed to take the white Eldorado to the garage that afternoon? Destiny just couldn't remember.

Thank God the drapes were drawn. She knew that a couple of the other neighborhood women in Brentwood — wonderful, smart, intelligent women like Destiny who were pillars of the community and had once chaired PTA committees at the all-white schools — had mammoth telescopic lenses aimed constantly at her estate. They hoped to catch a glimpse of the poolman undressing or some sort of voyeuristic rubbish. Well, take a good look, girls. Take a look at a forty-year-old survivor pouring herself a drink in her flawlessly decorated Colonial mansion at 9:30 in the morning and wearing her raspberry robe designed exclusively for this moment by Bill Blass.

It was like a World War III of gossip in Brentwood each day. A group of soap-opera fans had formed a civil patrol and their main preoccupation was dredging up the trash of each resident. The group reported regularly around the chic-but-not-too-chic tables at the private beach club down on Pacific Coast Highway. Destiny called it Casa de Garbage.

Underwear fetishes were very big that year. Destiny knew all about it. She had once compiled all the seedy psychological ailments of her charming, Waspish, climbing, not-yet-at-the-top-but-almost-there neighbors. She had used a thick address book, a gift from her karate partner at a nearby figure salon, and by each name had listed their various hang-ups.

The A's were easy. Marilyn Ashman was the only name in the A's, and her name was underlined three times with thick black ink.

Destiny had first met Marilyn, an ash-blonde, golden survivoress in the Super Strata Sweepstakes, at Elizabeth Arden's while they were both having their legs waxed. But Marilyn was not doing any favors for her husband. Ms. Ashman was into blacks. Preferably jocks. Couldn't get enough.

Destiny's manicured fingernails turned to the C's: CAROLINE CLARK.

Honey blonde. Beautiful. Big tits. A champion ice skater. But everyone knew the truth about Mrs. Clark. She was a former Sunset Strip hooker. She had first greeted her current husband at her studio of prostitution in the Hollywood Hills. Typically, he was totally frustrated about his sexuality. He had attempted the missionary position for years and never really gotten off on it. But once he met Caroline he regained his lost masculinity. She had one profit-making plan in those hustling days. Give the customer self-confidence. So when her current partner in life, a construction tycoon, had produced a portie toilet and asked Caroline to watch him as he defecated she had howled with delight. They had become inseparable ever since.

There used to be standards. But now it was a whole

new enchilada. There was so much going on with Destiny's friends. Much more than needlework courses and cooking classes.

Of course most of the women in Destiny's set were considered respectable. They took care of their children. Watched over their spouses' careers. Joyfully performed the menial chores required of them as suburban, affluent, elite wives. Joined the right clubs. They were attractive, healthy, college educated, reasonably well-off, living fashionably in what they agreed was the best of all possible environments. But, like Destiny, they were bored. Receiving those devastating locked-in vibes.

Destiny glanced at her gold Rolex watch, a wedding anniversary gift from her husband, who was away that weekend attending an insurance convention. Ten thirty. She remembered an appointment. A group of women, some of the more presentable of her set, were meeting at noon at Rainbow's End.

Destiny did not cherish the thought of three women, all of them bored to death with stories about real estate and sex, gathering at the greatest hen party in the West. But, in a perverse way, she relished the excitement. She had once watched an old MGM movie on television which showed Nero's mistresses' headquarters in marvelous Metrocolor. Rainbow's End always reminded her of such a Hollywood version of a Roman harem. Every woman at the restaurant competed for the attention of the group. Some through clothes. Some through outlandish coiffures. Others with well-preserved beauty. But mostly through loudness. Whoever shouted the strongest over the din in the heartstoppingly beautiful restaurant, which was supposed to inspire visions of Vienna, was awarded the gold star of the day. But Rainbow's End was absolutely safe. Husbands did not mind paying the outlandish prices and women were allowed to drink too much and stick around until five or so barreling out divorce stories. Destiny almost enjoyed the spectacle of slipping youth and fading beauty. Until she caught a glimpse of herself in one of the overdecorated mirrors.

That reminded her. Destiny made a mental note. She would not put on a pound at lunch. Not an ounce. Weight, as well as everything else that had to do with her body, was becoming a problem. Her hairdresser at Neiman-Marcus had explained that as she aged gravity was to become her main opponent. For vast sums of money he spent hours applying makeup and cutting her hair so that her face would turn charmingly upward, giving her the youthful appearance of an aging movie queen. But the beauty treatments weren't producing the proper results. Destiny no longer looked thirty. Or even a matronly thirty-five. She looked her age. That was definitely not done in Brentwood.

Eating, of course, was no fun anymore. It was that dangerous time of life. Not only was Destiny going through a spiritual crisis, but her body, which had once been voluptuous, if somewhat thin-hipped, was sagging. The final condemnation of her predicament had come from her thoughtful mother. She had sympathetically purchased a posture strap from a drugstore to correct her daughter's blossoming dowager hump. Destiny had already attempted adult braces.

Destiny waged a campaign against anyone under forty. She hated the sight of her teenage daughter, a sweet girl. She had even given up dope. But everything about her sixteen-year-old reeked of sensuality and youth. And all of those baby sitters. They were walking trouble. She watched her husband as his eyes devoured them. Sophistication, wit, and being a wonderful companion just weren't enough. Maybe she could get a rejuvenation shot in Yugoslavia. But Destiny wouldn't think about that today. Thinking, her analyst had informed her, was absolutely the worst thing she could do in her condition.

Destiny switched on the stereo. She found some jazz, uninhibited voices chanting about "lookin' so good" and "shake it, baby, shake it." That was *good* therapy. She prepared to descend into her private fantasy bathroom, decked out like a movie star's dressing room with flashing lights and miraculous bottles of perfume and cosmetics. Another day. Another face. She would be perfect. Everyone said she resembled Rhonda Fleming.

Destiny loved materialism. She devoured affluence. She always said her life was so much better than her parents', who told her horror stories of the Great Depression. To hell with all these boring women who had discovered themselves and were out to transform the world. All they had was neurosis. For Destiny there was absolutely nothing wrong with comfort. Being able to go into any fine store and purchase what she desired. Having the choice of coming home to a house that was elegant, where she could hold dinner parties and entertain charming people. Nice clothes to wear. She had absolute faith in her womanliness.

Another thing, what's wrong with *winners?* She was not aligned with those women she knew who met the husband at the door and relayed disaster stories of maids quitting. Not for Destiny. She subscribed to the theory that she was selling satisfaction to her husband. She treated him as the supreme head of the home because he *was* the breadwinner.

Destiny's ideas might have been considered old hat, and *Ms.* magazine had never selected her as one of the prophets of the eighties. However, she still had a husband. That's more than she could say for many of the other restless paradise seekers in Brentwood.

Destiny decided on her Chanel suit. That ought to scare the hell out of those other bitches.

Well, what was she going to do?

Patricia, a tall, svelte, well-dressed, thirty-one-year-old woman whom many people sized up as good Junior League material, parked her gray BMW in the parking lot of the Westward Ho supermarket in downtown Brentwood. She didn't *need* anything. Who was she going to buy for? There was no one at the palace. Her husband, whom Patricia thought of as the gentle jock, had left her for a younger woman. Younger being twenty-four. The kids — two — had been packed and sent to Patricia's mother in San Francisco. This was a major moment in Patricia's career as a Brentwood wife. At noon she would be attending her last lunch.

Patricia was familiar with the rules. Once the divorce papers were filed you became a threat. There was only one way to become reinstated in the club. Become a married woman again. Not only that, but she would have to find a man with taste, with a bulging wallet, and with some talent. Most men she knew didn't have the proper credentials.

So what was Patricia going to do? Like most Brentwood women her social circles were somewhat removed from the glamorous Beverly Hills shampoo set. Patricia had never been properly introduced to Hollywood producers or movie stars. Well, she did know Margaret O'Brien, the one-time child star. But who remembered her anymore?

The men that Patricia now dated were certainly rich. Yet something had happened to available male material in

Brentwood. They seemed to prefer dope to women. The doctors and lawyers wanted her to toot and snort and find them dope dealers. Patricia had found herself in the company of friends of friends who were in from New York on business deals looking for some California action. Her only successful affair since the divorce was with the nineteen-year-old son of her pediatrician. Sometimes he performed mime tricks. Adorable. But he would not come up to snuff as marriage material.

Patricia could produce high-quality sex. Everybody said she was a solid lady, and the money she would be receiving from her husband in the divorce settlement was enormous. But when Patricia entered her friends' houses she could tell something was... different. She was a divorcée. A threat. The enemy.

Patricia was not sure what to do with her life. What was worse, she had sexual fantasies at the oddest moments. For the first time in her life Patricia had begun leafing through the centerfolds of *Playgirl* at the Vendome — a better-than-average gourmet liquor store. The models were much too pretty and slightly boyish. She knew it wasn't the tasteful thing to do. At night the beautiful men appeared in her dreams. Patricia had become fascinated by the folds at the crotch of the worsted suits of the models and the pink photographs of what lay beneath.

Patricia discovered herself fantasizing as a rich array of men marched to and fro from their sports cars in the parking lot to the electric doors of the supermarket. In and out. Out and in. Brentwood was an amusement park of men. Patricia had never completely let go. Now she was imagining all sorts of things. She suddenly wanted to make love to the policeman astride his gleaming motorcycle, with the fat, fatherly man at the delicatessen section of the market who always gave her extra helpings of potato salad, with the blond checkstand boy. Dick was good. She wanted to scribble it on her windshield for the world to see. But Patricia didn't know how to make the first move. Where to go? How to get it on?

She couldn't just sit here all day. There were things to do. She started the car. Attempted to smile at the men crossing her path. Infrequently one of them noticed the desperation in her eyes.

My God, what was happening to her? Her life was wonderful. She had everything. The dreamhouse, the California hideaway in the hills with the pool and the Picassos and the gardeners three times a week. She had tried tennis. Joined a pyramid party. Visited her shrink once a week. But her life wasn't working. Now that she was divorced it did no good to cook like crazy or subscribe to travel magazines to keep up with the latest luxe resort. Maybe, Patricia thought, somebody was out there who would pass by some night, see the light in the window, and make her life perfect again.

But what was she going to do? Patricia would have to become an adult lady. She drove to Wilshire Boulevard, the main throughfare in El Lay connecting Santa Monica, Westwood, Brentwood, and Beverly Hills. She practically went insane.

The towering, monolithic office buildings were in full bloom. Lunch hour. From every revolving door came hundreds of attractive, fashionable, three-piece-suited wonders. Men. Patricia pulled her Diane von Furstenberg sunglasses from the visor and put them on.

Kiss. Kiss.

Carole was late. Destiny and Patricia were already seated at the Rainbow's End bar. But Carole didn't give a damn what the other Brentwood wives thought. She was still glowing from the quickie on the beach with the construction worker. It had been better than Deborah Kerr and Burt Lancaster in the torrid love scene in *From Here to Eternity*. For a moment she almost forgot herself. She could wait a few minutes before devouring the male beauty show of gorgeous waiters and bartenders in the elegant Brentwood restaurant.

Destiny offered her left cheek for the social kiss. She was actually considering how magnificent Carole looked that afternoon. But Destiny didn't look bad either. She had already examined every pore and was flattered that the low-lit interiors of the restaurant had produced amazing results. She looked thirty-five. Her Chanel suit had been a definite win. Already the Mexican-American car attendant had checked her out. Destiny was familiar with the stories about the South-of-the-Border romances in Beverly Hills. How many of the upper-crust wives had simply let go, allowing those Latin lovers to seduce them in the back seats of their Eldorados. But Destiny wasn't preoccupied with sex. Maybe she would investigate a face lift. That would be something to do.

Patricia offered her best profile to be pecked by Carole in the time-honored tradition of the California social pack. Patricia was already on her second glass of white wine. It was not a good sign. Then it happened. Patricia had spotted a remarkably attractive, tall, dark-haired, three-piece-suited businessman at one of the better tables and undressed him at least three times in her unexpurgated daydreams. Patricia flirted wildly.

Something was missing, of course. The three women would act out their Cinderella dreams of being all dressed up and having someplace to go. Like the other women and assorted men of various social importance at the extravagant million-dollar luncheon spot they had been told they would have to wait for their table. But you could only exchange comments about the weather and the kids and make everything at home sound divine just so long.

Eating, naturally, was passé. For about three years no one who was anyone in Brentwood had eaten a decent meal. Fashion had dictated thinness. Nobody accepted an invitation for lunch at Rainbow's End to eat. They came because it was an event. This is where women who had made their fortunes through marriage came for the gossip and the trashy conversations. If you were pushing forty and still well preserved you saw a shrink, made a reservation for a facial at Georgette Klinger's on Rodeo, and had lunch once a week at Rainbow's End. It became the thing to do.

Carole ordered her first white wine from the bartender and arranged her hair in the gold-leaf mirrors of the bar. Well, here she was in the entertainment capital of the world. At the big party in the Golden West. She felt horny.

Destiny was concerned about Patricia. Now that Patricia was a divorcée Destiny realized it would be the proper thing to do to arrange a dinner party and find some attractive, single men for Patricia. But she didn't know anybody terrific. She decided, instead, to compliment Patricia on her tan. It was something to say.

After another long twenty minutes, the Brentwood women were shown to their table in the open-air garden area, from which they had an opportunity to see who was there that afternoon and to overhear any juicy tidbits they were saying.

"Oh, there's the contessa." Carole's trained eyes picked up the travels of a bizarre, carrot-haired woman dressed in volumes of rainbow-colored designer knits who was table-hopping through the interiors of the restaurant. She was a local legend. A socially prominent woman who had become a landmark by spending thousands to throw herself a coronation in Beverly Hills a few years back. She wasn't really a contessa. Her name was Alice Cohn, and she was a housewife with a voice like Dodie Goodman's. But in Beverly Hills Alice didn't live there anymore. They all wanted to be royalty. Even if they had to put it on their license plates.

Carole's attention, however, quickly switched from the social lioness to more interesting material. Carole was searching for men. The perfect lay. Flirtation was very big with the Rainbow's End bunch. Carole didn't care if the only available catch seemed to be the 104-year-old tycoon driven into the restaurant in a wheelchair.

Patricia had also experienced a near thrill. One of the bus boys, the one with the perfect 10 ass, had brushed her arm casually. Patricia had read *Body Language*. She knew what that meant. Immediately her mood changed from depression to optimism.

All these G.D. plants. Carole was sick of the lushness. But she perked up when she located three unescorted men at a rear table near the fountains in the garden. One of them looked Italian. The other probably Arabian. The third was an obvious homosexual. My God, black leather drag at Rainbow's End. Well, it *was* California.

Destiny watched Carole working the room and admired her perfect teeth, the exquisite nose job, the full breasts. Old urges rose in Destiny. She hated these undeclared tendencies. She feared them. Taking a sip of her white wine she studied Patricia. She watched Patricia demolish her salad. The young ones had enormous appetites. Destiny felt a tremor inside her. She reached into her Gucci bag for a cigarette. She undid the first two buttons of her Chanel jacket. It *was* hot that day.

Carole took a spoon from the perfect table setting and

placed it against a sparkling goblet and made a toast to her friends. But she was thinking how uptight these Brentwood babes had become. She wasn't advocating that they all jump on fourteen mattresses in an orgy. But what was the use of fretting about maintaining your youth? Sex made you young.

When the waiter arrived with additional rolls she grabbed his leg, rubbed his thick calf muscles, and smiled. The waiter returned the smile, displaying a delicious set of sparkling teeth. Carole let her eyes fall slowly, intentionally to his fly and licked her lips. She wished she had worn her see-through blouse.

Carole needed a quickie. She excused herself from the group to visit the powder room. She waited at the bar, out of the sight of her friends, and caught the eye of the waiter. Those tight, black trousers brought back memories of John Travolta in *Saturday Night Fever*. The waiter's eyes rested on her face. He seemed to know the score. Contact.

Rainbow's End was a difficult location for a seduction. The powder rooms were filled with elegant women trashing the other guests. The main floor a spectacle of conspicuous consumption. But when the waiter pushed the gilded doors of the kitchen apart and his eyes met Carole's she decided instantly to go for the gusto.

The kitchen was noisy and full of the aroma of soufflés. The staff were not disturbed by Carole's presence. The waiter motioned for her to enter a private dressing room.

The waiter was just a kid. Though totally hot. All hands. When it was over Carole found her voice and, as a surprise for her friends, ordered a chocolate soufflé for dessert. The waiter's hands tightened so hard around her small, gold Gucci bracelet that they were almost cutting into her wrist. Carole slowly returned to the bar.

She could have done a number on herself and made herself feel guilty. But it was funny. She felt no wrongdoing. She was very happily married to this wonderful man. Her kids were terrific. She actually felt good about the fact that she was now eating correctly. Life was perfect.

Carole saw ten people she knew in the restaurant. All women. She would have lunch with them all soon. It was something to do.

Patricia and Destiny had not missed her. Destiny had placed her hand on Patricia's in a maternal manner. Maybe the two of them would make it that afternoon, Carole thought. Or maybe all three of them.

There was supposed to be all this gold out here in California. Yet it was getting tougher. Carole wasn't one of those dizzy women who sat around looking beautiful, hoping somebody had dope or coke or something expensive to get her through the day. She was one of the Brentwood ladies.

Carole aimed a merry wave of her bejeweled arm in the direction of her group in the sun. It was all so perfect. Maybe she should take up prayer.

2 THE RELIGION

Honk your horn if you love Jesus. The "Let's Boogie" van pulled into the drive-in religious sanctuary for Sunday services that sun-kissed morning. The couple in the van were Orange County regulars. They resembled Dale Evans and Roy Rogers. She wore a bouffant hairdo and a lime and white, peppermint-striped pantsuit. He wore the latest in leisure suits, a denim job, which looked as if it had been borrowed from a used-car salesman down the sun-bleached boulevard.

There was a traffic jam for the car-culture pews. But nobody cared. This drive-in religion thing was big. Dr. Robert Schuller, its founder, had not only attracted the masses and celebrities like Frank Sinatra and Doris Day but had officiated at Hubert Humphrey's nationally televised funeral. Schuller had, praise be to God, built the $14-million Crystal Cathedral bigger than Notre Dame in Paris.

Well, Little Miss Orange County, about five-foot-four and cute as a button, and Mr. Macho Orange County, with a mustache, Mr. America pectorals, and totally into this Jesus thing to boot, had changed their lifestyle. Like some residents of the White House, they had gone the Born-Again route. Before conversion, they had been into recreational vehicles and dirt bikes in the desert. That was all over, those let's-do-it-in-the-dirt days. They had seen the glory from the windshields.

One day the van couple had been out cruising in Garden Grove, California, a bottom-of-the-pit, High Tack town of 80,000 or so in the vast frontierland of Southern California near Disneyland. There they had been struck by the most awesome sight of their life. It reminded them of a set from *The Empire Strikes Back*. Both of them were stoned out of their minds on home-grown Laguna Beach grass.

Suddenly, not far from a 7–11 fast-food store and a Pup 'n Taco Acapulco gold-colored hot-dog stand shaped like a plastic Swiss chalet, there appeared the Crystal Cathedral, a totally mirrored monstrosity, which looked like something they had seen in the pages of the *Whole Earth Catalog* — but bigger, much bigger — and it rose in the flatland spaces around the tract-home paradises like a space ship. "Jesus," Mr. Macho Orange County said to his cutie-pie, who was munching on a Hostess cupcake at the time, "it's *Close Encounters of the Third Kind*."

Hordes of tourists, other car-culture adventurers out for a day of fun in the sun, had also stopped to observe the architectural phenomenon. Japanese tour buses, filled with miniature businessmen dressed in white shirts, ties, and tailored wool-blend trousers, were lined up for blocks. Instamatics popped. Some of the more devout fell to their knees and began praying.

"What is it?" Mr. Macho Orange County asked one of the spectators, a woman dressed in the latest Orange County style — a powder pink princess dress with a fifties Elizabeth Taylor hairstyle and a cross as a comb.

"It's drive-in religion," she answered, her eyes reaching for the heaven above.

They steered the van, a citrus orange beauty, inside the huge compound. It felt so peaceful. But it was unlike any church they could remember. There were 2000 parking spaces, built in the exact style of California drive-in movie theaters.

The interior seemed more like a national park than a church. Someone, some ding-dong gardener, had filled the gardens with bird of paradise flowers and sculptured hedges.

The worshipers strolling inside the gardens, although straightforward folk who probably read the *Saturday Evening Post* and shopped for days at J. C. Penney's, had Born-Again smiles on their faces. There were several new California species which the young van couple had never encountered before. Everybody was friendly. Positive. Filled with polyester inspiration. Chimes tolled, filling the sanctified stillness with the sounds of "The Old Rugged Cross." In front of the van couple, next to the dazzling drive-in cathedral, stood a fourteen-story neon cross. Amazing.

It was the most important moment in the young couple's courtship. They had heard of the Jesus thing, but never experienced it before. They decided it might be a great club to join.

Sunday morning service was even more fantastic. The young couple parked the van on a stiff incline and set the emergency brake. You didn't want to have your car drift back and collide with the other worshipers singing hymns at the steering wheels in their cars.

A young usher whose golden hair was truly blinding passed them a church bulletin through a front window. As usual the young couple was responding in a positive way to the messages of inspiration within the bulletin. The woman turned the dial of the car radio to 540 KC, and they held hands while the church chorus on the drive-in loudspeaker sang upbeat, sunny hymns.

The scene before them was currently broadcast to 2 million worldwide TV-religious-hour fans in places like Sydney, Australia, and the Philippines and Puerto Rico, as well as inspiration seekers in the United States and California. The program, "The Hour of Power," had from the very beginning, back in 1968, been popular. How could electronic religion miss? The TV cameras aimed at the drive-in congregation, their multicolored cars basking in the gleam of the sun, and telecast scenes of nature from the gardens of the cathedral which rivaled the most cheery Hallmark cards.

But that was nothing compared to being there. Schuller, the most famous parking-lot padre in America, walked outside the Crystal Cathedral and glass walls parted like nothing since a Hollywood version of the Red Sea. Twelve fountains, one for each apostle, sprung skyward as Schuller beamed his message of eternal glow. "This is the day that God has made," exulted the fifty-five-year-old, silver-haired, drive-in preacher. "Let us be glad and rejoice in it."

Between Schuller's sermonettes, thanks to the presence of the TV cameras, things never got boring as they did in those other hell-and-damnation churches in Orange County. There were beach-boy rock-'n-roll bands — usually two sun-sensibility young men and one Olivia Newton-John look-alike — who rocked out for Jesus. For the older crowd — the senior citizens or keen-agers, as Schuller referred to them — who sat in their recreational vehicles sporting "We visited Yellowstone National Park" bumper stickers, there was also the Christian version of vaudeville. Norma Zimmer, the latest Lawrence Welk champagne girl, would use her powerful TV soprano to bring the crowds to tears.

The church organs were unbelievable. One of them had been purchased by the Reverend Schuller for $100,000 from Avery Fisher Hall in New York's Lincoln Center. The other was equally famous. You didn't merely attend church when you worshiped at Schuller's Garden Grove Community Church, you were watching a full-scale Broadway show at what was conversationally called the fastest-growing indoor/outdoor religious institution in the world.

By the time the ushers arrived at your vehicle for tithes and offerings, you had also heard from a Hollywood celebrity confessing how drive-in religion had released him from the Sodom and Gomorrah of fame and fortune. It literally poured from the confessionals at the pulpit. Doris Day. Rhonda Fleming. Glenn Ford. Even Ruth Carter Stapleton, the ex-President's sister, had come clean at Schuller's command. It was the best soap opera on Sunday morning TV religious hours.

Then Dr. Schuller bounded up to the pulpit and began pressing buttons for the dancing waters. You couldn't actually see the waters from your car, but there was a wonderful commotion on the loudspeakers. The spectators inside were going into ecstasy.

Schuller was dressed in crimson robes. But people didn't remember the robes. They remembered the smile. The sparkling, I've-seen-God-and-he-is-terrific eyes. Schuller never used a prepared sermon. He believed in spontaneous delivery and he was a born actor. They didn't give Emmy awards to TV preachers, or Most Promising Newcomer plaques to God's messengers, but Schuller's revival style of preaching was as explosive as a rock act. He thundered like Charlton Heston playing Moses. He raised his hands, the velvet sleeves of his preacher robes, and the drive-in sanctuary was calmed to silence.

Schuller was an Iowa farmboy who had decided to follow the ministry at four. He had been inspired by an uncle, one of Christ's missionaries to the heathens in China. When Schuller had chanced upon Orange County back in 1955, it seemed like the perfect place to plant seeds. So he personally rang 3500 doorbells of the modest, garden-blessed homes in the area and learned that the inhabitants loved two things — TV and cars.

Around Schuller's neck hung a gold medallion. Its slogan represented the main focus of his philosophy, a low-rent version of Dr. Norman Vincent Peale's *Power of Positive Thinking*. Schuller's version was dubbed Possibility Thinking. "A Possibility Thinker," according to the inscription on the medallion that was being worn in high places everywhere that year, "is a person who, when faced with a mountain, does not quit. He keeps on striving until he climbs over, finds a pass through, tunnels underneath, or simply stays and turns his mountain into a gold mine with God's help. A Possibility Thinker looks for all the possibilities in every situation instead of the impossibilities." It was very big in California that summer.

Not everyone could dream up a drive-in church. Or could induce the multitudes to bless him with $10 million per annum. One day the idea of religion via loudspeaker simply popped into his mind. Why not? The snack bar could be the pulpit. The refreshment stand the baptismal room. The middle-class, family-oriented burghers of Orange County relished new concepts. It was one of the fastest-growing areas in the United States and the home of such all-American attractions as Disneyland, the Movie Star Wax Museum, Knott's Berry Farm — an old boysenberry ranch which had been bulldozed to provide space for the log rides and the Debbie Reynolds concerts — and Lion Country

Safari. It had become the test tube of the hinterlands. Not as well entrenched with the trend makers as the rich arena of Los Angeles to the north, but rising... rising.

Orange County needed a religious leader. Not some old country-boy slick-o like Billy Graham. Kathryn Kulman and Reverend Ike were much too R-rated for mass culture, traditional tastes. They wanted a religious Barry Goldwater. They got Dr. Schuller.

Reverend Schuller realized what Orange County wanted. To lead the country back to God and peach pie. To send off powerful vibrations that could raise the nation from its deep sleep, wash away the sins and cynicism of Watergate. The Orange County middle class would be attracted to the values of the 1950s dressed up in space-age, technological trimmings. Affluence. Spirituality. Sunny smiles. Wouldn't it be wonderful?

Dr. Schuller was like the American flag to them. Christian. Successful. Businesslike. Brooks Brothers. Positive. Healthy. Clean. *Up.*

The couples in the drive-in congregation were often moved to tears by Schuller's inspiring messages. Sometimes they even turned on the windshield wipers in their more devastated moments. They always got what they came to hear. That in the common folk of Orange County lived the saviors of American morality. That hundreds of years from now the whole world would have heard about the fantastic events in Garden Grove. That even if they came from a hick town, and shopped in mammoth prefab shopping centers, and did their hair all wrong, were faced at home with the kids on drugs, and alcoholism, and their jobs were filled with worry and boredom, their troubles would vanish if they believed in the possibilities offered by instant car-culture religion.

It kind of hit you where you lived. Especially if you were like the van couple, totally lost in the anonymity of suburban life and unaware until Schuller that they were actually the new nobility, magnificent enough to worship in the $14-million Crystal Cathedral. The grassroots hadn't heard about the beauty of the common man to this extent since Roosevelt lifted them out of the Depression.

Back on stage, Dr. Schuller worked the majestic cathedral, as the dancing waters rose and the evangelical choirs sang hosannas from on high. The services were simultaneously translated into five languages. Four thousand seated worshipers filled the hall with divine applause. They *loved* the church. It was theirs. It was modern, open, more talked about than any religious building since Westminster Abbey. The cathedral was not only solar powered, but ecologically air-conditioned by the sea breezes of the region.

For couples like the van sweethearts it presented the most astounding mural in their rearview mirrors The couple, as well as the other members of the 10,000-strong church, *loved* the cathedral. The two of them had given Dr. Schuller $500 the previous summer in order to become members of the Pillar of Steel Club. They had received a beautiful certificate, to hang on a wall at home, that acknowledged their membership in the group of 16,500 other Possibility Thinkers who had raised the lacy steel framework of the cathedral.

Dr. Schuller had sent them a color rendition of the cathedral. The message enclosed reminded them that their children, as well as their children's children, would remember them as founding builders of the great center of drive-in religion. Five hundred dollars seemed a bargain price for immortality.

They were no longer nobodies, but somebodies. The compound was filled with reporters and sociologists studying their every moment. Stories about them and their church appeared in *Time, Newsweek, People,* the *Saturday Evening Post, Us, Now, Success Unlimited, New West,* and *Vogue.* The architect of Schuller's dream palace, Philip Johnson, was a cover boy on *Time* magazine. The members of the church consorted with the most talented, most honored architects. The "Today Show" had given viewers across America progress reports on the wonder of religious wonders. In 1955 Dr. Schuller had begun his ministry by climbing atop the rusty roof of a snack bar in an Orange County drive-in movie theater. There were eleven cars in attendance. Schuller had $200 to his name. Now he was being invited to the White House and performing for millions from his own version of Chartres.

There were five services that Sunday. The biggie being the 9:30 A.M. service, since that was when the crowds got to see themselves smiling and praying on television. Hardly anyone at Schuller's cathedral wanted to be baptized at any other hour. Because if they got baptized at the 9:30 service people all over the world would see the TV cameras zoom in on them as they knelt to meet their maker and smile the smile of self-esteem as Dr. Schuller, resplendent in his robes, anointed them with the Biblical waters.

That had been another major moment in the lives of the van couple. Coast-to-coast baptism. They had held a party for their friends the day their baptism was telecast. And were presented with a videotape of the proceedings by their best friends, also advocates of Schullerism.

Often the couple would arrive for the early 7:30 service and remain until sunset to hear the last service; it reminded them of Easter sunrise services or a religious holiday on the church campus, which Dr. Schuller referred to as a 250-acre shopping center for Christ.

There was fresh-perked coffee served by the lay ministry. Much to ponder. For each week Schuller devised another trinket for them to take home and fill their walls with joyful wisdom. That Sunday it was a miniature wooden boomerang which read, "Blessings Always Boomerang." For $7 they could attend classes at the drive-in educational facilities in such varied subjects as Growing Through Grief or a course called To Bind Up the Broken Hearted ("National coordinator of Suiciders Anonymous shares insights into depression — how to recognize it, accept it, and move on to positive Christianity").

There was usually some new game introduced at the church. Not pinball or any of your Las Vegas card tricks or slot machines — that would be sacrilegious — but what passed for services in the eighties breeding ground of electronic religion. If anything was troubling a member of the parish, there was a twenty-four-hour crisis line for which one would dial 714 and the words NEW HOPE. Vast Sunday school facilities were provided so that the children could play with miniature cars on the carpets while they watched Dr. Schuller on television. One could, if one wished, take tours of the TV production facilities, which were more sophisticated than many Hollywood sound stages. Or review a few of the 40,000 letters which poured in each week, addressed only to Dr. Robert Schuller, Garden Grove, California.

Mostly the van couple wanted to kick back in their car, crank up the volume dial on their car radio, and cassette tape-record all of Dr. Schuller's sermons. The speeches, which they played for inspiration while driving the freeways, frequently contained an uplifting theme. Schuller's brand of religion didn't focus much on Jesus or Scripture or any of the more traditional preaching methods. Instead, the good doctor prepared his flock for the anxiety and depression of daily life by lifting them above their worries to an imaginary level where all their dreams would come true. They could have anything they wanted, as long as they believed. One of the couple's favorite tapes was currently climbing on the Schuller hit parade. It was called "Turn Your Scars into Stars."

Everyone was treated royally at Schuller's religious drive-in resort. Reverend Schuller was not only a theology freak but a connoisseur of the latest developments in California's rich human potential movement. Esalen met TV religion at the Crystal Cathedral. Not only were the multitudes fed Sunday school stories, and incredible arrays of musical entertainment, but the latest psychobabble of the California transformation movement.

The congregation appeared so ordinary — so "Father Know Best" TV situation comedy squeaky clean. Yet they were being fed the basic California soma drugs of total joy. Through the message of the soul administered by Schuller and his huge staff the van couple had moved from self-doubt to self-confidence. From self-condemnation to self-effectiveness, self-acceptance, and self-love. They would drive into the compound unconscious, but Schuller, who often screamed as if he had received the word from God that instant, woke them up and charged them with holding the banners for The American Way of Life.

The van couple always kept Windex inside their glove compartment when they attended Sunday services. Sometimes flies and bugs splattered the windshield and ruined the view of Schuller as he stepped out onto the cement patio and blessed the cars.

They no longer did drugs. After a sermon from Schuller they were amazingly high — and they would drive to lunch or breakfast at the nearby coffee shops with plastic white roosters atop the thatch roofs and share their good will with their lost neighbors.

Nobody knew the truth about Dr. Schuller. Some of the more liberated members of the laity had wondered just what was going on underneath those crimson velvet robes. There were rumors in religious circles that the good doctor got up every morning and hollered out his front door: "I feel happy, healthy, and terrific." The underground gossip network also reported that Schuller had "happy spells" all the time, and would stand on tiptoe, quivering with be-here-and-now joy. Of course he had been visited by God many times. But then, who hadn't?

Schuller never resorted to laying-on-of-hands tricks. Or rode into services atop a white horse, as some of his California religious brothers had done. Schuller didn't buy the old gimmicks of American revivalists. To Schuller Jesus was the greatest psychologist of all time. Growth, that was the ticket. Why was everyone leaving the church in droves? Schuller thought the flight was connected to hell-and-damnation fundamentalism. He was not interested in that. Schuller not only intended to be the Lawrence Welk of TV religion but also the Dear Abby of the silver chalice set.

That Sunday morning, while the congregation queued up waiting for the gates to open for church, Schuller rose early in his three-bedroom home in Orange, just a few freeway exits from the cathedral. He was greeted by his Ultra-Brite wife of thirty years, Arvella, who, according to articles in Christian monthlies, did all the ironing, washing, and cooking and still contributed forty hours a week for her "church duties." The Schullers shared the family home, their Laguna Beach apartment, and their Lake Arrowhead mountain cabin with their five children. There were no *down* moods, as Schuller described them, around the fireside at the Schuller home. When faced with an angry child given to tantrums, Schuller simply informed the child that his radio was receiving a bad station and asked him to dial to a more positive program. It was nothing like *The Exorcist*.

Schuller would jump — he never walked, but bounded, jogged, or flew — into his brown Cadillac Seville for the pleasant ride to the sanctuary. Pink Cadillacs were no longer in style for Southern California religious leaders that year. But neither were VW Rabbits. The plush, comfortable automobile — like many of Schuller's possessions — was a gift from one of his parish members, who told the *New York Times* that a Great Man like the father of drive-in religion shouldn't have to ride around in just any gas-eater.

Schuller tooled down the freeways, his face lit up like a searchlight, seemingly tranquil. Recently his reputation had reached a new apex, the network TV breakthrough — he had conducted Hubert Humphrey's nationally broadcast funeral. Billy Graham may still be at the top of the religious charts, but Schuller was number two with a bullet.

Schuller was the TV prophet of good times. There was enough vengeance on the six o'clock news. Maybe Marvin Hamlisch would write a musical about his life. Perhaps Julie Andrews could play his wife. Schuller told reporters he was holding out for John Denver to recreate him on the silver screen.

The good people of Orange County applauded him as he entered the huge religious compound. Some yearned to touch his robes. School children lined up around the entranceways to the church, telling their parents they hoped to see a good man once in their lives. They wanted to see what a good man *looked like*.

What a scene. Schuller in his Cadillac zooming up to his parking space near the Crystal Cathedral. Then, to the cheers of the congregation as for a football hero, the glass doors parted and he would rise high above the throngs to a tune that sounded like a Christian version of *Thus Spake Zarathustra*.

A little organ music, please. Some Max Factor pancake makeup to erase the slightest imperfection on the brow of the TV culture hero. Quick shots of California clouds and trees swaying in harmonious winds for the vast television audience. Schuller's market research had shown that unless you used quick cuts viewers would get bored and move on to other religious programs.

Zoom in on a little safe sex appeal. Schuller may not be Hugh Hefner, but he did have a healthy Madonna complex. There was a big TV market of men like Schuller who appreciated the simple, wholesome beauty of the supermarket, schoolteacher, homemaker sex symbols in the choir. Schuller's Angels, some called them.

Dr. Schuller on stage had managed to amplify religion. It was small-screen ecstasy held just at the brink of orgasm.

For an hour birds chirped, Schuller preached, celebrities (today, Mickey Rooney) confessed, and Schuller forgave every transgression, casting such a golden light of goodness on the throngs that his show was one of the highest-rated TV hours on Sunday morning.

The car-culture congregation in the Drive-In Sanctuary, as well as the peasants dialing in via satellite in Mexico, listened to Schuller's voice washing over them, caressing them. The good doctor looked into their eyes from his side of the TV cameras, and he had so much he wanted to tell them. So much.

3 BOYS TOWN - THE WEEKEND

FRIDAY

Paradise was one of the living immortals to the word *m-a-c-h-o*. Like everyone else in the world of gay life, Hollywood's homosexuals had enshrined his name everywhere. So it should not have surprised Paradise that his arrival in Boys Town created almost as large a furor as Anita Bryant arriving for a religious crusade. Paradise was famous for his menacing, faintly dangerous air, which was portrayed in super-realistic images on billboard advertisements throughout America. Without even trying, he had become one of the top commercial male models in the world. His lean, bronzed body exuded the very aura of maleness. He moved with the fluid grace of a panther stalking the jungle. He had perhaps the loveliest thighs in the animal kingdom.

The gay world was having a love affair, watching with aesthetic joy each new arrival of his billboard adventures. Paradise high in the Rockies mountain climbing. Paradise on an outrigger in Hawaii. Paradise going back to nature in the green fields of the American heartland, smiling his smile of cocksure maleness. But the only thing Paradise was not sure of was his sexuality.

Paradise, like everyone else, had his own reasons for arriving at the sunburned gates of Boys Town. He wanted to become a star. He hadn't been in Hollywood twenty-four hours before he had found himself in an agent's office on the Sunset Strip. The agent, an ex–tennis player, now worked for a large international agency in an office tower complete with wall-to-wall secretarial pools and classy clients demanding up to $5 million per film. It was obvious after fifteen minutes of conversation that the agent felt the strength of America lay in its youth. He spent his spare time helping wayward boys. Helping them any way he could.

The agent was also a classic closet case. He quickly pointed out to Paradise Hollywood's homophobic attitudes. American women did not want their cinematic superstuds caught in any indelicate gay scandals. If Paradise became a star, the agent explained, he would be expected to arrive at important Hollywood events with a woman on his arm — at all times. The agent told Paradise about one famous Hollywood gay couple — two producers — who had lived together for thirty years and still took separate limousines to important parties. No bars. No baths. It had become Hollywood's eleventh commandment.

Paradise lit a thick joint of sensimillia grass. He had heard of California's famous home-grown grass, imported from the fields of hippie communes in Northern California. Now he toked on the joint in his friend's mission-style home in the Hollywood Hills above Boys Town. Paradise was trying his best to lose his New York energy and become part of the mañana mentality.

The home was on a hilly acre. He counted the natural wonders. The gardens were planted with camellias, azaleas, an avocado and a peach tree, birds of paradise, a lemon tree, and a patch of carnations. The interiors of the home, owned by a gay photographer who shot most of the covers for male-order catalogs, reflected Hollywood homosexual taste. A huge painting of a can of Crisco dominated the wall of the living room, which was stocked with exotic plants and Polynesian furniture. It was the perfect setting to relax. Paradise, however, could not unwind.

Paradise was a sexual retard. He possessed pure physical beauty. Few male bodies were ever so exquisite: the glistening copper skin, the elegant cheekbones, the easy curvatures, the lithe frame, the entire grace. But every time Paradise was about to reach out for the sexual ecstasy that should have been his at command, a yellow light went off in his brain.

When the panic button was pressed, Paradise fled. Southern California was gleaming outside that day: smogless, picture-postcard beauty. Paradise, dressed in gym shorts and shirtless, found the silvery van in the driveway. Vans, his photographer friend had advised him, were a blessing to the gays of Boys Town. Curbside sex was very popular that summer. He might as well get some sun, Paradise thought. See what was going on inside the perfect world outside.

Paradise's territory up to now had been the grit and grime of New York's East Side. But as the van moved silently along the streets flooded with two-story palms and perpetual blue skies he found himself in a densely populated tropical jungle of exaggerated pastel mansions featuring tinkling fountains and wrought-iron balconies.

Then he saw him. Paradise was not alone in his travels through Boys Town for long. At one of the ubiquitous corners of the city — the one with the prerequisite service station and the last drive-in restaurant in the Southern California flatlands — Paradise spotted a hitchhiker. A respectable, all-American, blue-eyed Boy Next Door — if the neighborhood happened to be Utopia.

The boy had just returned from a two-day trip to somewhere in suburbia with someone he had met hitchhiking. He told Paradise that he had learned to live on nothing. Friends supplied him with dope and drink. A kindly older acquaintance had supplied him with a rent-free apartment. He was always in the gym, lifting weights or busy in the steam room. He was headed for a little park down on Robertson Boulevard, where young men sunned bare-chested while they worked out in an outdoor gymnasium.

The young man instructed Paradise to drive to Griffith Park, a huge hillside playland inhabited by gays that year. The boy said he was not sure he was gay. So the yellow caution light immediately vanished from Paradise's interior control panels.

The boy was enthusiastically open, like everyone else Paradise had encountered in Southern California. He looked naive. But he knew the ropes of Boys Town. On the journey through the residential and commercial neighborhoods adjoining Griffith Park he pointed out the local landmarks. Santa Monica Boulevard, also known as the Great Gay Way, with its corner hustlers — young men with gaps in their teeth and tattoos on their arms. The leather bars along Melrose Avenue, where slave bracelets were sold as well as Guard, the first gay douche. ("Be prepared for anything . . . anywhere.") Silver Lake, the low-rent mountainside retreat, where gay couples were into leather and western.

The van moved with the heavy traffic into a community know as Los Feliz, the Beverly Hills of gaydom. Paradise was amazed at the mansions that lined the wide streets. The boy explained that most of the homes were owned by gays. The boy pointed to a monstrous, castle-like estate, complete with moats and baronial balconies. The butyl nitrate king lived there. No one had ever seen him. He never left his home. His pool parties were famous. His orgy rooms were envied.

Los Angeles was a boom town to many of the gay population. They had turned their fetishes into fortunes.

Paradise struggled to erase the idea of erotica from his head. He concentrated instead on the beauty of Griffith Park beyond the van's windshield. The rich flora and fauna. The shady groves. The little brooks and waterfalls.

The boy studied Paradise and was pleased. He had come to Eden to find an Adam or Eve. Paradise was the closest he had come to the moneyed, beautiful ghosts of his daydreams. His body was boy-lean, flat-bellied, and narrow-hipped. The only difference between Paradise and himself was that there was more of Paradise. He would play it cool. But the moment would arrive when he would play his cards. There were no caution lights as far as he was concerned. All signals said go.

Blackie Norton would be remembered as the disco daddy. There was money to be made in Boys Town. Blackie Norton had most of it. Blackie was the leader of the local Gay Mafia. The gay Godfather. When there was a dollar to be made, Blackie was around. He had his feelers out for any gay enterprise, no matter how shoddy.

Blackie was the man behind Ciro's West, the most famous gay disco nightclub in the world. It represented quite an achievement. Blackie had single-handedly dissolved the dark-lit seaminess of former gay underworld palaces and provided a dance hall campus for the clean-cut, blond, California-squeaky-clean boys who arrived in Hollywood to become atmosphere in movie beach epics. Ciro's West rivaled Moulin Rouge in Paris. The floor show of dancers each night provided visitors to California's gay ghetto a vision of a merry-go-round of beauty amidst the flashing disco arc lights.

Blackie was very attractive — a quality new to gay businessmen in Boys Town, who in the past tended to look like either dyed poodles or Skid Row alcoholics. Blackie was tall and had blue eyes and dark hair. Some of his best enemies admitted he looked like a soap opera prince. At thirty-two he dressed casually, aping the youth style of California. Blackie was rich. Many people wanted to be around his energy. Only a few penetrated his businesslike facade.

Everyone wanted to meet Blackie Norton. He could certify the uncertifiable "in." Held the key to the most magical parties in the gay universe. No one wanted to get on the bad side of Blackie Norton. His mother had always said that he was born to be burned. Black gays, whom Blackie sometimes barred from Ciro's West, had nicknamed him B-A-D. Nothing stood in the way of Blackie's greed. He wanted every boy who danced at Ciro's West and he wanted every cent in his Gucci pocketbook.

Blackie was at his post at Ciro's West that weekend, watching the action on the dance floor. He lived with only one fear. That the Los Angeles Police Department would bust his palace. The police department regularly conducted pogroms of mass brutality in Boys Town. So far Blackie had toed the line. But the police were waiting for him to make one false move. Blackie paid generously for his freedom from the vice squad. But who didn't?

Blackie was a hero. Gay libbers said that Blackie had brought gayness out into the open and provided a showcase for heterosexuals to experience the bright side of homosexuality. But Blackie did not care about the crown of Wonder Gay. He was much too materialistic for such acknowledgments. Blackie dreamed of riches beyond the wildest imagination. He desired a kingdom of his own, populated by a cast of thousands at his command. The gays would kiss his ring.

Blackie had a soft spot. He was one of the last of the romantics. But Blackie was still searching for the real thing. A man who would knock him over the head with his penis and put him in a state of unconsciousness for two hours. A real man. Not too many appeared at Ciro's West.

Blackie watched the dancers who crowded Friday night at Ciro's West. A magazine columnist had written that the disco looked like a Roman fresco of male, mostly topless torsos engaging in battle. Sweat was the perfume of the night. There were no mirrors on the dance floor. The dancers peered into the mirrors of the other dancers to see if they had passed the test. If, on a scale from one to five, they rated a five.

Was there life after dark in Los Angeles? The disco fad was dying. But not with gays. Ciro's West and Circus and Studio One, the four-star gay disco palaces, still packed them in each night. Starting around four on balmy afternoons what Blackie called the gay clones would primp and preen and take to the streets. They drove splashy Porsches and customized Jeeps, the ones with the spread-eagle customized jobs. Toyota trucks were also chic.

Bar-hopping was a must. The Blue Parrot on Santa Monica Boulevard in the heart of Boys Town had begun a trend to upgrading the gay bar image in El Lay. In the Blue Parrot, also known as the Plastic Parrot, the rich and famous mingled with the desperate and the pathetic to drink and to fondle their way through tropical nights. Blackie, as well as all the other members of El Lay's lavender generation, picked up the latest styles at the Blue Parrot. Heard the newest gay expressions. There were jungle paintings of plants on the bar's exotically colored walls. The atmosphere was dark. The music pounding and sensual. Someone, some inspired genius, had even added the perfect touch — a raised platform center stage where trick after trick spent a few moments surveying the crowds and offering themselves as slaves to their lust.

There were no closets in the Blue Parrot. The bar and its clientele were open to the traffic passing by on Santa Monica Boulevard, to the shoppers going for drag at Ah Men (the boutique with the *best* posing strap collection) and for Boy Next Door gear at the Sports Locker, a gay sporting-goods emporium which did a huge business selling customized jock straps.

This was Blackie Norton's status-conscious world. The world of the U.G.'s (Upper Gays). There was an L.G. (Lower Gay) netherworld farther east on Santa Monica Boulevard, where the proletarian gay community of Boys Town sniffed poppers and smoked dope in the back rooms of magnetic, masculine-flavored cabarets. Blackie, however, ran a class act. He was the prototype for the West Hollywood success model. He did not travel down the road. Only up. Climbing in El Lay's gay circles was an art.

Blackie was not Robert Redford. Still, he was considered quite a catch. There was a kind of honor system in Ciro's West. A contest each night to determine which dancer Blackie would select from the masses of couples dancing their asses off on the moonbeam-lit dance floor. The disc jockey would play fast songs and slow, romantic ballads. The big question in the men's room was always, Who would Blackie pick as tonight's pin-up boy?

Trick had never danced at Ciro's West before. But he knew the game. As he strode confidently to the dance floor he turned to his best friend and told him that he'd have

Blackie Norton on his knees in a back room of Ciro's West in ten minutes.

Trick was a rarity in the Boys Town world of the new morality. The perfect gay. Gayness ran from the top of his thick, blond fluffy, princely haircut to the very toes of his Nike tennis shoes. Trick could make entrances. He could make exits. Trick could make men drool.

Gay historians allege that God usually gave only one such enticing beauty, one such sexual being, to each new gay generation. Few were aware that Trick was the grandson of a Los Angeles blueblood socialite and had attended private boarding schools in Switzerland. What most people noticed was a gay surfer with a living end and a full crotch, itching, it seemed, for more action than Casanova.

Trick was built to be banal. The way he danced was remembered. He would not disrobe on the dance floor — that was a turn-off. Trick had extravagant tastes. He splished and splashed on the dance floor. People noticed.

Blackie Norton did not spot Trick immediately. He had been distracted by a blond ski instructor from Aspen who was wearing a down jacket and hiking boots. This had to be heaven. The full, red lips like lollipops. The tight designer jeans and throbbing well-built physique.

Then Blackie's eyes met Trick's. It was like a dream sequence in a Hollywood musical. The crowds vanished in a dreamy haze and the two men locked together in a visual embrace. It happened like that in Boys Town. Blackie Norton was on his knees in a back room in exactly ten minutes.

They called him Liberty, as well as other things. The Black Beauty was big. Sometimes the Black Guy. Everybody swore that Liberty was straight. A raving heterosexual. After all, he had become one of the most famous athletes of the era. A household word. The media packaged him in every conceivable way. Not always with aplomb. Liberty was getting better. But he could hardly be bigger.

Photographers said that he must have used Michelangelo as a role model. Super-masculine. Skin the color of See's Candy. A body manufactured by coaches to parade before the TV masses and make them bow to his glorious image.

Black athletes had broken all the barriers to interracial fantasies in America. Liberty entered the bedrooms of the rich and the powerful and the elite. Was invited to attend their status ceremonies. Placed on their best-dressed lists. Allowed to romance their patrician daughters. However, Liberty didn't care for women. He found them amusing; when it came to erotica he wanted men.

Boys Town was off limits to athletes. The few gay sports figures who had declared themselves homosexuals had lost points in the world that mattered. They had become media freaks. Oddities. It was tragic. But it was reality. Liberty realized that Boys Town was a ghetto. Beautiful and tropical and fascinating and wild. But there were no exits. Liberty had promised himself that he would never fully lose his identity to the homosexual underworld. He would remain on the fringes. Millions of dollars were at stake.

Boys Town had the best meat rack in El Lay. Liberty had traveled all over the world and around it a couple of times. Yet he had never seen a show like this on any other city street. Like other gays, he often cruised Robertson Boulevard past the decorator-row, awning-drenched antique shops to the main street of Boys Town. Liberty would turn right on Santa Monica Boulevard in his Mercedes 450 SL and watch the street show as the leather boys and the drag queens competed on the sidewalks.

There was something tribal about it. Fleets of hitchhikers, thumbs out and poised for action, lined Santa Monica Boulevard at all hours of the day and night. Liberty could hear the upbeat music pouring from the bars. The nights were warm. Many of the street people had their own cruising territories. Many wore short haircuts, Levi's, and black motorcycle boots. They didn't walk. They swished. They didn't talk. They screamed. They didn't make it in the movies. But they inspired the streets. It was the gay world.

Liberty entered the X-rated motel room in Hollywood, just east of Boys Town. He liked this particular motor hotel because the owners didn't ask questions and it was private. The rooms were clean, though not grand. The bedspread was crimson red. Gold-leaf mirrors had been placed at the head of the bed and overhead so that one could watch while making love. The television set did not offer programs listed in *TV Guide.*

Liberty needed love. Sex. His schedule had been a constant rush for the last month. He showered and rubbed some mineral oil on his trim, wonderful frame. He wrapped a towel around his waist, the way he had dressed in so many locker rooms after games, and walked to the living room to use the phone.

Therapeutic massage from student athlete. Get high, kick back, and get off. At your house, hotel, or office.

He had found the ad in one of the porno newspapers sold from racks throughout Los Angeles. It wasn't a popular gay journal like *The Advocate,* which published its own sex listings called Trader Dick's. That would have been too chancy. Liberty preferred the discretion of finding partners in straight porno papers which featured a few gay-oriented advertisements between the eat-my-pussy masseuse ads and the X-rated movie reviews.

The telephone conversation was brief. The boy wanted $70 an hour. He would arrive at the motel in a half-hour. Addresses and phone numbers were exchanged. Liberty had been aroused by the boy's voice. He was a big kid — six-foot-two, blond, blue-eyed, hung, and husky.

There was nothing effeminate about Liberty. He was gay. But he was virile. His body was not only beautiful but graceful. His musculature incomparable. Liberty was tough. He liked to wrestle. He did not prefer soft males. He did not like gentle sex. He wasn't a sadist, not that he knew. But inside he felt like a warrior. He did battle with the boys whom he paid for sex.

Liberty positioned himself atop the velvet bedspread of the waterbed and removed the towel. He glanced down at his family jewels. Stevie Wonder music was playing on the wall stereo in the motel. Liberty felt like a samurai. They practiced sex differently in Boys Town than in Japan. But erotic adventure had been raised to a level of high art. He was expecting great pleasure.

When the boy arrived Liberty was not disappointed. They made love in front of the fireplace like gladiators. Liberty knew the boy had recognized him. The boy realized that Liberty knew. But no one else would know. One thing about hustlers — they didn't gossip.

4 THE HUSTLER

4:00 P.M., BEVERLY HILLS

STEWART WAS ANAL. That was the word he used to describe his condition that afternoon — a condition of constant constipation of the spirit which came from the fact that he was in Beverly Hills and he was not making it. Stewart was thirty, and as every salesgirl and even most of the Beverly Hills lesbian population (which was incredibly large and very active) would tell him, he was "beautiful." In a town that fell to its knees over movie stars, Stewart possessed the kind of movieland gloss and glitz that caused women to linger lovingly as they sorted out each recognizable beauty mark. The brown hair was fine and cut in the athletic style of Nick Nolte. The all-American face was tanned and saved from adorableness by the finely contoured cheeks and the cold, honest brown eyes. He seemed to the women who paid $100 an hour ($200 overnight) like a bored Burt Reynolds. He dressed casually for a male prostitute, but with care — selecting tight, form-fitting jeans and billowing sport shirts in colors which were subtly masculine.

Prince Charmings were very big in Beverly Hills. Each

woman felt she had the right to mate with such creatures as Stewart. Yet they couldn't quite figure him out. He wasn't one of the dandies who strolled down the spotlessly clean sidewalks awaiting fashion photographers' flashes or slowly taking in the displays of Paris-approved menswear in the immaculately designed windows at Jerry Magnin's. He wasn't a hip businessman carting cocaine and stocks in status briefcases, marching like charm-school models into the sumptuous, chandeliered banks along Wilshire. He wasn't even a modern fuzzy wuzzy, driving a Jeep, mellowed out with self-improvement courses, desiring an "enlightened" romance, and, of course, dinner for two at the Ginger Man. No, when women hit on Stewart they found themselves drawn to the fact that he assumed no airs of self-importance, no lunchtime Ma Maison manners, no gigolo drawing-room-comedy, Cary Grant charm, no phony charisma. Stewart had a straightforwardness which, mixed with his English-boarding-school manners, simply sent women up the walls. There was something about him — probably that cool detachment — that encouraged fantasies in women of a man who would cause no problems, could dispense all the amenities, and bring them to multiple orgasms with marvelous ease.

So beautiful and yet so lost. They would all want to mama him, wrap him in the ultra-current clothes of say, Maxfield Bleu, and await with pleasure undressing him and watching his totally tanned manhood move stoically and cleanly through the fantasyland of all the sex scenes in those novels tucked conveniently under their movie-star-fantasy beds. Here was one man that didn't need an electric dildo. Stewart was the kind of man that women in Beverly Hills liked to watch stepping out of their shower. His hair slicked back and wet. The water dribbling over each rich, tanned crevice of his ultra-glamorous, designer-jeans-commercial body. But they could never reach him. Never possess him completely. Women enjoyed the mystery of Stewart — the fact that he got down to business without ever boring them with autobiographical stories. He was orderly, prompt, perfect, and always seemed brand new. They could buy him the way they ordered $200 vials of Bal à Versailles perfume at Giorgio's on Rodeo. He seemed to fit their package-deal sensibility. The perfect male toy.

It wasn't that Stewart wasn't passionate. He was incredibly passionate. He lusted for every single accoutrement of the untotaled pleasure that the city offered. Beverly Hills was a bejeweled candy store to Stewart. It represented style and class and money and bullshit. He delighted in the spectacle of it all. He could remember that ten years ago this master-planned village was just a sleepy little resort. European aristocracy visited Beverly Hills for a tan, but they never treated it seriously as an international playground. Today streets like Rodeo Drive rivaled the rue du Faubourg in Paris and Bond Street in London. The eccentricities of current fashion were carried to an extreme. The women had the healthy, lanky bodies of ocean princesses and the looks of cover girls on *Vogue* and *Harper's Bazaar*. Tourists carrying their Instamatics and their movie-star maps shuffled along the gilded avenues openly worshiping the sights as if they had arrived at a status shrine. Their food consisted of the best haute cuisine. The shopping palaces were filled with $250,000 gold-encrusted, red-carpeted stairways. In such an environment, Stewart was valuable. Most of the men and women living in Beverly Hills had money, wit, charm, plastic surgeon looks. But they lacked beauty or youth. Most of them. Stewart, the haute hustler, was loaded with both. Besides that, he knew all there was to know about silk crêpe de Chine. In Beverly Hills, *that* was important. Stewart had grown up in Beverly Hills.

Stewart's favorite memories were of the times his mother would lend him the white Rolls-Royce in which he glided up and down the avenues waiting for THE LOOK. The rich, gray womb of the sweet-smelling interior of the classic automobile caused him to flash back on his childhood — a time when such luxury was taken for granted and Stewart was treated as the little prince whose every wish was granted. The trips to movie-star estates to lock the finely crafted doors with monstrous crests and start a really serious game of "doctor" came flashing back like old wounds. On his first day of school in Beverly Hills Stewart, like the other children living in this rarefied world, had been dropped off in a Rolls. He remembered being certain that the thing he wanted most in all the world was to be exactly like his father. Stewart could easily remember his father — tall, golden, impeccable — escorting him to school. That trip seemed as frozen in his memory as a religious painting, bathed in golds and fuzzy, because his father was magic. He made everything seem larger than life. He lived for pizzazz. He raised Stewart to inherit the earth.

There was only one thing wrong with this production. His father was running an old reel from *Citizen Kane*. He was self-righteous about his wealth, and he came from the school of tyrant who expected children finally to make their own fortune in the world. On the day Stewart finished high school — the very day that he had run a Gucci jock strap up the school flagpole — Stewart's wonderful, stingy father died. There were no more lavish parties thrown by the studios for the children. There were no more Rolls-Royces waiting at the school exits. No more boarding schools where Stewart was trained like a Pakistani prince to treasure fine,

fine women and a lavish lifestyle. His father had left him a little something — but nothing like what Stewart needed to survive in the golden jungle. His father had never given Stewart the minibike he craved at twelve. Now he left him nearly penniless, working as a waiter at the Saloon and peddling his flesh to the readers of *Scruples*.

Sensing failure, Stewart had fled Beverly Hills. He had attempted to find himself by growing his hair the length of a rock star's, by dropping acid until he turned comatose, and by studying meditation with the Maharishi in India. But his movie wasn't *Easy Rider,* it was more like *Shampoo*. History was not taking place in the hinterlands. It was happening in his own backyard. When he returned home to Beverly Hills everything was more splendid than he had remembered. The endless sun. The crimson sunsets igniting the mirrored office buildings. The wide streets lined with trees cut like forests from *Alice in Wonderland*. The boutiques, displaying status labels on their candy-striped awnings like perfume bottles, were crowded with rich foreigners. The newly rich — the kind that worked days and played all night — had inherited the forty-four-room mansions and the flamingo-filled lagoon-like playpens. It seemed to Stewart like a city which had poured magnums of champagne and cartons of caviar on its citizenry and baked them until they were a rich Acapulco gold.

It was then that Stewart realized that the city was truly anal. A bitch. Stewart peered at himself in the rearview mirror of his tacky red Triumph sports car (a gift from an admirer of the late Jacqueline Susann) and admitted the truth. He had been trained to live this life. His father had taught him about fine wine, dope, and women. Fine toys. Then he left Stewart with nothing. The city had become a ghetto in which hustlers like Stewart needed to be surrounded by refinement the way movie audiences craved Sensurround. There was no exit, until Hollywood invented it. The American Dream had been within Stewart's grasp, and then it vanished.

Very few people realized Stewart's sadness. He hid it and his intelligence beneath a bored facade that blended with his environment. When he would hang out at the Ginger Man to listen to co-owner Carroll O'Connor ("Hey, Archie Bunker") play the piano for his guests, he seemed glamour incarnate. He also made the rounds at Carlos 'n Charlie's discotheque on the Sunset Strip, using a card he filched from a rich South American customer of young flesh. Women in tight leopard-print jumpsuits and Carioca white dresses would buy him brandy and soak up his body on the dance floor. Underneath all this posing, Stewart was romantic. At night he returned to his apartment ($500 a month furnished) in the tacky, lower end of Beverly Hills and stretched out in his luxurious Spanish bed, smoked a joint, and dreamed of a girl who might be rich, sensitive, affectionate, warm, and would immediately sense that he wasn't a hustler. Someone who could make some kind of difference in the world.

When the telephone rang, the caller would be a woman, wasted on Quaaludes or uppers, saying that Stewart had been referred to her and that she might want to get together with him that evening. Stewart knew all his clients' questions by heart. What did he look like? Six-foot-two, green eyes, brown hair, forty-four-inch shoulders, twenty-eight-inch waist, tanned, and he liked to have a good time. Most of the women pressed for more information of a vital nature. Stewart never lied. Did he like to eat them out? Yes. Did he like anal intercourse? Whatever you dig, baby. Did he have any grass or drugs? Anything you like, sweetheart.

Stewart was a class prostitute. He could provide a "safe space" for women to experience their fantasies and everything he offered was agreeable. There were days when he would make seven calls. Each client was listed in a black book by his telephone — name, number, her preferences in bed, in drinks, and in drugs. Each woman would be called on a regular basis so that Stewart could depend on a certain stable to pay his rent and bills. He drew the line at S & M and bondage — but anything else was okay as far as he was concerned. His clients: a sixteen-year-old heiress who played the soundtrack of *Grease* endlessly and visited Stewart in his apartment but had to be home by midnight to return her parents' Porsche; a fifty-six-year-old divorced woman playwright who read him chapters from her forthcoming script about the sexual exploits of Beverly Hills housewives. This woman, who practiced transcendental meditation and went to a $900-a-week ashram in the San Fernando Valley to get in touch with herself, had Stewart reenact each scene of her play in the bedroom and played a cassette of each of their sessions the next day for material for her novels. Many of the calls Stewart received were out of curiosity — but he had prostitution down to a science. He *never* spent more than three minutes on the phone with a client and would bring the sale to a close by asking: "So, when shall we get together?" Almost always in their homes, the date set by a telephone call. Women who were too afraid to chance an encounter met him at the Beverly Hills Hotel lobby and tucked an envelope with $100 into his jeans pocket. This entitled them to call for several hours of what Stewart dubbed "fantasy phone calls." One of the leading socialites of the city, a woman who could buy and sell most of the other residents, was fond of masturbating while listening to Stewart on her Princess telephone as he brought her to a climax with his voice. Some of the women were incredibly beautiful. Most of them were not. Stewart could write volumes on fat, baldness, old age, and cottage-cheese thighs. Stewart never went on an appointment without taking a shower and without stuffing a bottle of butyl nitrate inside his sleek trousers. He would have the women inhale the tangerine-colored, pungent liquid, bringing them to highs of ecstasy in which they called his name while they gyrated on their silk sheets. He was like a surgeon with the clients. Quick, incisive gestures — aimed at bringing them to a climax. No appointment lasted longer than an hour, and most times women would fill that time just talking about their endless problems with husbands, lovers, and friends. Stewart fit into Beverly Hills life like a fancy caterer. He provided a service. What had he learned about these Beverly Hills women in their queen-sized homes and their soap opera existence? They lusted for attention. Many of the women brought him gifts — watches, clothes, extra money. However, most of them handled him by credit card, passing him off as a masseur. As a lunch guest.

When telephone business was off Stewart knew exactly where to go to make an extra $100 or so. To the pool of a Beverly Hills hotel, where the suites cost $200 a day and the pool was filled with young divorcées who would throw their Vuitton luggage on the luxe carpets with glee and scamper down to poolside in their Norma Kamali cut-out swimsuits to enjoy the only game in town — lust. Stewart would park near the hotel, remove his clothes in his car, and then, presto — a nylon Speedo brief swimsuit over his powerfully built, grade AAA frame, a frame built like a Ferrari at the posh European boarding schools — glide in bronzed splendor to the pool. He knew he had it made.

Stewart was on a down curve from a joint he had smoked a half-hour earlier, and he was enjoying the panorama set before him. The hotel had a classic reputation as a prim and proper establishment. Yet around the pool Stewart was reminded of a Fellini movie he had once seen in boarding school. This was the home of THE LOOK. And each woman who stepped before him would pause, look into his camera, and wait for a flash of recognition, as if life were a cameo in a movie magazine. The scene was bizarre. Many of the women had wrapped their heads in rainbow-colored knit scarves tied in the style of the twenties movie-star mating gear. Most of them held tight (even while tanning) to a status bag, as if without that bag their whole position in life would crash around them like sputtering fireworks. This was the show that Stewart enjoyed. On the streets of the city and even by the pool there was an air of pretentiousness that was a constant source of amusement to one as worldly as Stewart. All the types paraded by him. The young cunt — with an expression of benevolent boredom — in the tightest swimsuit, who walked through the maze as if she sensed that there wasn't enough air freshener in the world. The old but successful women in the one-piece suits with incredible stripes that made them look like serene zebras. The tight-assed secretaries from the Midwest who carried themselves as if they were posing for Kotex commercials and who kept their eyes lowered, watching the pools of water on the hot cement.

These were not the women Stewart pursued. His eyes darted from white lounge chair to white lounge chair, looking for younger, well-maintained women who shared his amusement at the manners and mores of waterhole eleganza. Women who understood that they were attending a performance in the outdoor theaters of Beverly Hills. Such women usually wore exaggerated sunglasses, form-fitting swimsuits, and looked as if they were living DO NOT DISTURB signs. Stewart had no fear of women. He knew that Beverly Hills was nothing more than a huge beauty spa. That most of the women had been massaged and toned down and given immaculate haircuts — royal treatments — during the day and were now ready for the party. There was one type Stewart avoided. The not-so-rich posing as rich. They were, as Stewart put it, a page from the age. Beverly Hills was loaded with such folks, just as Paris had had its run on phony artists. Stewart could spot them easily because they waited for THE LOOK much too long — maybe a full minute — and when they did get it, they would smirk for the rest of the afternoon. To such people, Beverly Hills was a game. They had come dressed in denim and workshirts and soon traded them in for the latest uniform from the smart shops. Beverly Hills loved such types.

Stewart felt an itch in his crotch. It was time to begin the party. He rose gracefully from his lounge chair and moved to the pool. Waiting until every tinted eyelash was pointed in his direction he plunged into the pool, his massive frame causing water to spray the poolside regulars. He swam like Jon Hall in *Hurricane*. Swift, smooth strokes, each one more cleverly conceived because he was high. Stoked. He swam ten laps of the pool before raising himself like a gladiator onto the hot, pink pavement. He noticed that Miss Do Not Disturb had removed her sunglasses but still lay glacially in her chair. That was a good sign. He flashed his million-dollar smile as he walked toward her. Stewart had the same approach with all his prospective clients. He would love them and love them and love them. He would look for an asset — their legs, tan, hair, clothes — and begin by complimenting them repeatedly. He would be totally with them. That meant if he saw insecurity — the need for a daddy — he would play daddy. If they were bored and looking for someone outrageous Stewart would become completely off-the-wall. Stewart realized that everyone there wanted to play. And he massaged Miss Do Not Disturb with compliments. She turned out pretty much as Stewart had expected. A young woman with an older, although monumentally wealthy, husband. Stewart realized that the woman was aware of the fact that their encounter was being recorded by the other women poolside out of the side of their raccoon-like Aida Gray made-up eyes. He began rubbing sun gel over her back, carefully stroking her like a masseur until she purred.

"Do you want a joint?"

"Yes, for God's sake."

Miss Do Not Disturb was now throwing the door of her suite open, running inside like a small child at her grandest birthday party. She cranked up the upbeat music piped like air conditioning into her room, which was decorated like a contemporary art gallery in wild metallic aluminum and hot red colors. He produced a thin, finely rolled joint from his pack of Marlboros. It was Hawaiian Gold — not only a high, but an aphrodisiac that caused the smoker to gaze out on the world through a golden, sensuous prism. While they smoked he stroked. He made women feel like superstars in a marvelous movie in which all the cameras were directed on their every movement. He noticed the woman staring at his swimsuit, now full. He glanced at her as if to suggest that any fantasy was available. But he was a pro. "You realize, this will be exactly one hour," he told her. She understood that a price was to be paid. While the woman closed the drapes, Stewart finished the joint. She loosened her bra, then her tight bikini bottom. There could be no doubt she was beautiful — as probably Elizabeth Taylor had been beautiful. Voluptuous. Stewart began dancing;

she joined. Producing the vial of butyl nitrate, he took a deep, intoxicating snort. He kissed a scar under her belly button. She took the butyl nitrate bottle, holding it to her nose while she breathed deeply. "Let loose, baby," Stewart commanded. He worked his blue swimsuit like a male dancer in a boylesque joint. When he was naked, they danced closely together, Stewart rubbing his manhood in every crevice of her femininity.

Stewart carried the woman to her bed, far up the stairs and to the right. Looking into her eyes, he could sense that this woman wanted it slow and she wanted it hard and she wanted it to last and last.

For a moment he stood above her, smiling. She pulled him down into the sweet air of sachets provided by maid service. The music pounded in the background like a sensuous chorus, and the late sun falling on the red wallpaper sent blushes of pink across their bodies. It all went very slowly. Very beautifully. His strong arms enfolded her body. Her hands slid up and down his body, counting the muscles, feeling each bulge of flesh. She sighed. Stewart existed off other people's fantasies.

For the woman, this was temporarily the end of boredom. The climax of her day, a day of routines of which she had long since tired — the shopping, the makeup, the exercise, the late lunches at the Bistro. She had only come to the hotel for the weekend for *this*. She did not want it to end. But Stewart's sexuality lasted only as long as the top-rated TV newsmagazine, "60 Minutes." Like a Las Vegas entertainer, he had to rest and prepare for another show. There were others by the pool who had seen him move in on the woman, and they were tasting rich fantasies of their own as they broiled in the tropical sun. As he showered, the woman watched him. She reached for her Hermes purse, the kind she knew Princess Grace carried on royal functions. She wrapped a $100 bill around the vial of butyl nitrate with a rubber band and rose to look at herself in the ornate mirror facing the bed. First, she studied her tan, then let her eyes cruise her figure. She began making plans for dinner. She felt glowing.

Stewart walked out of the hotel into the warm, sultry night. Beverly Hills at night. A few tourists parading up and down the thoroughfares, dreaming fantasies of being caught in a magnificent picture book and turning the pages as they pause before each shop window. Black limousines with blacked-out passenger windows buzzed sleekly into the torchlight parade of automobile lights. Two crazy girls — dressed up as Air Force Wafs — cruised him and asked him for a light. The town had shut down under the tinsel-perfect blaze of a full moon. He had always searched for a metaphor for the city. Now he was close. Beverly Hills was simply a rich Disneyland. A game. Everyone was a hustler. He stuffed the butyl nitrate into his trouser pocket, placed the $100 bill in his bag. A tourist yelled from a car, "Look, there's Ryan O'Neal." And his friend called back, "No, that's nobody."

5 THE HOSTESS

10:00 P.M., WEST HOLLYWOOD

THE HOUSE WAS TUDOR, of course. A big, gray affair hidden by a forest of trees and located in *not* the best neighborhood. But still everybody came to the parties thrown by Dana Magnin there. Dana Magnin? Well, of course she had that name. The department store Magnin name. She had been married to Jerry, the youngest scion of the Cyril Magnin litter. Now, Dana was divorcing him. Something about another woman or something bogus like that. She was free, thirty-one, blonde, and she wore silk dresses that clung to her form (rather thin, but appealing). Her hair fell around her porcelain pretty face as if it were fresh from a shipwreck at sea. The *Titanic,* she called the look.

Every week, it seemed, Dana was giving a party for forty or so. "Last week it was the Governor, this week a rock star, what's next, eh, Dana?" Buck Henry, the comedian and confidant of Warren Beatty (they co-directed *Heaven Can Wait*), was fond of whispering into her little-girl ear. There was something about Dana. Something that caused frequent guest, *Vogue*'s West Coast editor, Eleanore Phillips to ask, with one eyebrow arched in perpetual Hedda Hopper–like amazement, "Don't you think Dana ought to be in *House and Garden?*" Yes, *Vogue* was there. And everyone else who was young, trendy, climbing, opportuning, and busting loose from the regular Hollywood and Beverly Hills party circuit.

Dana's affairs were labeled fender-bumpers. Inside the house one group was dancing in the den, another drinking and getting loaded in the living room, which featured a mirror with the inscription: "This ain't no dress rehearsal, baby!" The rest of the gang-bang congregated in Dana's kitchen, a High Tech masterpiece, with copper skillets hanging from the ceiling and cheesecakes hidden in pink bakery cartons. Everybody busted loose from the regular social conventions at Dana's. People loved to visit her salon in West Hollywood because for once the celebrities could be caught with their facades down.

Everybody approached these parties itching for society column mention and waiting for the moment when they could rub elbows with Guvvy Jerry Brown ("I'll have a Tab, Dana") or body buddy Arnold Schwarzenegger, the biggest piece of superstar beefcake in town. Even the bisexuals present in abundance agreed sadly, "Arnold was straighter than the Arrow Collar ads." Bouncing down the stairs, sporting Mick Jagger hair, is Beverly Hills hairdresser to the stars, Carrie White, who cuts Bette Midler's locks. White was doing her famous imitation of Rita Moreno doing Bette Davis in her *Human Bondage* period. White actually drove a 1950 white Pontiac, a teenie classic in which she played New Wave cassettes and frequently cleared Sunset Boulevard when she yelled at passers-by: "I've got the best act in the city." A thin piece of dynamite, White didn't merely work Dana's parties — she attacked them like a social general. When things grew dull, she yelled an obscenity into the smoke-filled rooms or grabbed for yet another glass of vino under the perpetual candlelight. Or later in the evening related stories about how most other G.D. hairdressers in Hollywood copied her prophetic styles. "I should charge them for coming to me," she would bellow, like Olive Oyl condemning Popeye. "They pay for the entertainment when they come to me. I give the best floor show in Beverly Hills."

Peggy Pierrepont would laugh, but she had heard the story week after week. She was like a secretary to Dana's first-lady act. Part of Dana's entourage who arrived early to set the brandy in place, and stayed late to sweep the crumbs off the Indonesian rugs. The "in" group, including Peggy, would be invited up to Dana's bedroom. Dana would rush to the bedroom every half-hour, her cross between a Carol Channing–Tallulah Bankhead smoking voice babbling about makeup. "You see, I'm a natural girl," she said. "But you have to put makeup on for the rest of the women. I try so hard and see, it gets rubbed off with the hugging and the kissing. So, I'm constantly looking like the creature from the black lagoon. And I have to rush up here and get freshened up." Many of the guests thought Dana looked like Joanne Woodward coming up for air in one of those Faulkner family crazy movie melodramas on late-night TV. But Dana knew who she was. A space cadet. Anyone interested in space cadet training could apply at the door.

Downstairs, young women in colorful clothes would swing through the rooms, drinks in hand, voluminous forms swinging in the coolness of the California nights like metronomes gone beserk. Business deals were made at Dana's. A salon was provided for people to realize their fantasies. A movie producer, unsung and unknown, would regale a group with his plans to recreate the Anglo-Saxon empire, starring Richard Burton and Richard Harris.

An amazing twenty-four-year-old Newport Beach beauty

with blond hair and creamy, tan skin, dressed as a Borsalino type, described the latest episode in gay etiquette. He taught charm (of a new order) to the guests — gay or straight. "Now after you go swimming in the ocean," he instructed several fascinated onlookers, "make sure when you shower that you wash with soap only under your arms and your asshole. Men love the smell of the salt water. They will pounce on you in alleys." The beauty had weighed in at 250 pounds a year ago, but with the help of Arnold and the Studio One disco he had plummeted into a *Playgirl* centerfold. Dana loved him because if guests were boring he rushed up to them, listened for exactly one minute, then pronounced them "bogus," like Beau Brummel at an English court.

Dana was partial to thinking that anyone born in California after 1950 was blessed with the best incubation the world could offer. To her, California represented abundant air conditioning, incredible homes, the constant backdrop of history in the making, and the best dentists, plastic surgeons, gyms, spas, cultural courses, workshops that the world could offer at the moment. She drove a truck — her latest toy — at ninety miles per hour. She rattled narcissistically about the California dream.

Some of the women attending Dana's parties had strange names, names that sounded as though they had been invented for an Andy Warhol after-midnight movie. The Couture Queen, for instance, was semi-Swedish, and she supervised a high-gloss tanning salon. She always arrived looking like a Paris mannikin who had suffered from diet-pill fatigue. Couture Queen showed off the newest cultural experiments emanating from the California party set. She stuffed cigarettes (Winstons, one remembers) into a vial of Locker Room (liquid smelling salts), then distributed the cigarettes to her circle and waited girlishly for the moment they would unbend. She thrilled when she watched the guests catching the elite at their drugged-out best.

Dana was smart, everybody realized that. Her personal dream was to totally redesign the foremost cities of the Western world so that people could relate to each other. Many of her best friends considered Dana the Auntie Mame of the eighties. Dana was certainly a stroker. The type of woman who threw her pencil-thin, Snow White arms around guests, kissing them as if she hadn't seen them for centuries and immediately placing her personal seal of approval on their wildest schemes. She arranged her parties so that the most powerful men of all strata of the California scene were close at hand. She collected strays, her mother warned her. But often the strays turned out to be the shapers of the California dream. "Oh, no, Jerry Brown will never marry Linda Ronstadt," Dana would say. "The only reason he took her to Africa was to make sure she understood the way her life would change if she were First Lady."

Dana was certain she could never be California's First Lady. Three kids, for one thing. Two divorces another. Before Magnin she had been married to a man who had campaigned for mayor in San Francisco. In between marriages, Dana had conquered continents like South America and China, scouring out-of-the-way spots like Nicaragua and Taiwan for baskets. Dana Magnin credited herself with creating the basket craze that sent trendy housewives and Bloomingdale's buyers down to Africa to find just the right weave to chic up their plants.

Now she had turned her address into one of the new party-life retreats that were booming in El Lay. Everyone thought her parties were casual. But she picked her guest list like a playwright. She wanted to see the neon red-haired punk star enter with Debby Harry's choreographer. She wanted to see the fear on the guests' faces as social columnists moved within their battle zone and recorded for posterity the bon mots of the glitterati.

First-timers, having drunk too much, would whisper, "Have you screwed her? She must be hot. She must climb the walls up there. Look at her — she's like a Tennessee Williams heroine. A cat on a hot tin roof."

Not really. Dana had been an angelic Catholic schoolgirl in a parochial school in San Francisco. She had been a surfer girl playing with toys and boys on the beach. She had unleashed herself after two marriages to take the est training. It was almost as if Los Angeles had its first cultural gang leader. Dana's parties were like addictions. Every person you might expect to read about in *Rolling Stone* was on the guest list. And plied with liquor and delicacies so earthy that they felt just as though they were at home. As the guests unwound the secrets of El Lay became transparent. People found the fashion trends there. "Don't you think they'll be wearing zoot suits next year?" pondered a well-dressed woman. Hollywood's next epics were spawned here. "Don't you suppose the pod people would love Dana?" asked a million-dollar-a-year Hollywood publicist. Political trends were discussed. "They should call Jerry Brown Jerry Ronstadt." Limousines were parked outside, their drivers told to wait. Most of the guests were cultured, horny, and gorgeous. Dana had the best stable of young men — the most attractive, hand-picked at endless parties. Most of the women couldn't hold a candle to the Magnin magnificence, and they acknowledged that Dana was intelligent. She wouldn't create an orgy and offer too much competition.

This was no Madame Bovary scene. Dana Magnin wasn't playing the games of climbing. She loved being the party princess, the confidante of movie stars like Jane Fonda, who would call her from Utah asking her to chair her latest anti-nuke benefit. Adventuresses were riding the social waves of the El Lay circuit. She took care of her own. She supported their whacky desires. She bedded them, offering them her maternal breasts. Dana Magnin was a type. She wasn't a public spectacle like Régine, the Parisian disco queen. But a private spectacle. The nomads who moved to Hollywood in search of glory would remember her Fairfax house as the beginning of something. A break from the old order, a melange of lifestyles, a playpen noted in the social chronicles of the city.

Every week Dana went to a hospital for her chemotherapy treatment. Dana Magnin knew a lot about death. Now she intended to live.

6 BOYS TOWN – THE WEEKEND

SATURDAY

There had been no lovemaking. Paradise and the hitchhiker had stretched out in the back of the van the night before, the stars appearing outside. They had held each other and talked. Now it was early morning, and fishermen in their gray Windbreakers and thigh-high galoshes had arrived at the beach to silently mine the Pacific.

The boy had climbed back under the bright wool covers to sleep through the dawn. His name was Michael. Paradise studied his face. He looked like a preppie, his blond hair cut short in the style of students at Harvard and Stanford that year. Michael was wrapped in a down parka. He had a slight case of adolescent acne. Other than that, he seemed to have been born in Disneyland.

Paradise lit his first joint of the morning. He waited untill he was lost in the haze and his brain was floating, unraveling. Paradise couldn't quite fathom Boys Town. But he was in love. Michael had touched him. The boy spoke like a popular song. It was as if someone had given Michael's voice a guitar and he was producing the anthems of a new age.

Michael believed in a world that did not worry. He could see a future in which everyone would be free to touch each other openly. Where humanity was no longer afraid of its sensuality.

Paradise and Michael had made plans. They would live together, in one of those old Hollywood bungalows built in the thirties with poinsettias around its porches. Paradise would support the boy and watch him grow.

Paradise left the van. Draping a huge ski parka around himself he walked on the beach. He examined the small birds flitting to and fro on the wet sand. Witnessed with exhilaration the waves' motions at morning tide. There was a huge rock formation stretching out into the edges of the ocean. Paradise found himself at its tip watching the sea burst upon the rocks. This was the edge of the world. The end of the West.

Paradise could not get Michael out of his mind. The boy's ocean-foam blue eyes burned into his memory. When Paradise looked deep inside them, homosexuality did not seem wrong. But Paradise was not wise to the ways of Boys Town. He was simply a neophyte.

Boys Town was not a way of life but a game. Like Monopoly. Only the best players survived. Homosexuals lived by their own rules, but they died in the process. Not physically, but spiritually. The ones who made it in Boys Town had learned that life there was like the weather — accepted for what it was. Paradise could not comprehend the treachery. But he would be affected. You never knew what could happen to you during a weekend in Boys Town. Paradise decided to let it flow.

Blackie Norton woke late. Blackie was familiar with the game. Unless you were desperate and you hadn't found a trick on Friday night you didn't appear back on the streets of Boys Town until at least noon.

Blackie could hear the sound of Trick's blue Ford truck starting and watched from the window as the speck of beauty descended the mountain road outside his estate and returned to the delights of Santa Monica Boulevard.

Nothing was permanent. Trick knew the rules. He had played his role as boy beauty to the hilt. Given 100 percent. Blackie Norton had been provided with a rich night of sexual fantasy. Now it was over. There were no words to be spoken. No sad good-byes. If you were smart like Trick you never lived in the past. You left it out in the garbage pails to be picked up in the afternoon by Boys Town's maintenance men. The only important thing about the future was the sexual climbing. That the next romance was richer. More beautiful. A brighter star. Trick had received his sexual stroke and now anticipated higher forms of narcissistic entertainment. He had plans for a certain bisexual movie mogul.

Blackie Norton considered the boy for a moment. He knew that Trick had a reputation for gossip that equaled Truman Capote's. He realized that the boy would be telling stories of his night with Blackie Norton down in the bars and the open-air restaurants in Boys Town. But Blackie also knew that it was good public relations. More customers would be flocking to Ciro's West. More gay boys would be talking about Blackie Norton that day. It was called word-of-mouth.

Besides, Blackie had better things to do. There were much better shows in Boys Town than his bedroom, a spectacular glass-enclosed room which projected off the side of his wooden fairy-tale castle in the Hollywood Hills. Blackie dressed and decided to go to the gym.

Gay gyms were prospering in Boys Town. The best, the Bodycenter, was located on Third Street near the furniture district. The Bodycenter had become such an institution in the gay world that branches had also become established in Manhattan, Dallas, and San Francisco. Straight, heterosexual men had wandered inside the Bodycenter from time to time. But they soon tired of being grabbed on the ass in the showers. Women were not allowed inside the garden-like, High Tech locker rooms.

Blackie called the Bodycenter the U.G. (Upper Gay) gym. Not only did a horde of motion picture performers and their agents and publicists and television stars flex their muscles there, but from opening to closing throbbing music played, offering a sensuous backdrop for the workouts of the gay muscle boys.

Blackie was well aware that much more than Nautilus machines was pumping at the gym. Numerous important Hollywood deals had been signed at the Bodycenter. Many invitations to important parties were passed out in the locker rooms.

The Gay Mafia met in the steam rooms and the Jacuzzis. Some said the future of Boys Town was settled in the white tile showers. There was money to be made. Deals to be dealt. Opportunities to be explored. The Bodycenter was not just one of the most celebrated gay gymnasiums since the days of the Roman Empire. It was the first sign that Hollywood gays were ganging together to offer economic support for their own lifestyle.

Blackie would sit in the oakwood sauna and eat his heart out for the achingly beautiful men who had flocked to the Bodycenter. Yet Blackie was smart enough to have figured out that even the most spectacular of the males sweating it out for stardom had a price. It was his personal quest to find out just how much each gay man cost in Boys Town.

Liberty's friend was cooking a Judy Garland omelet in his *Meet Me in St. Louis* kitchen. His name was Shadow and he thought the word *boner* should come back. Shadow was very tired of *cock* and *dick*. Shadow flitted and flew through his hillside apartment, which was decorated in Early Barbra Streisand. Shadow was an advocate of Gay Musical Comedy Theater. He subscribed to the idea that *Auntie Mame* should be performed on Broadway in drag. Lots of costumes. Very Mike Todd.

Liberty was, according to homosexual jargon, a straight type. Men like Liberty found any signs of outward sexuality a put-off. Liberty had worshiped westerns as a child. *Rifleman* was a favorite. *The Big Valley*. Any John Wayne rerun. Liberty pictured himself as a black cowboy. He connected with virility. When he grew up and learned that a cowboy had a penis he was hooked. From that day in the movie theater when a stranger had seduced him while Rock Hudson rode the range, Liberty was gay.

Shadow was a star collector. If he couldn't screw them, he always told Liberty, he might as well watch them. Shadow loved gossip.

Trick often spent afternoons at Shadow's. Today he had the lowdown on Blackie Norton, and he couldn't wait to tell Shadow everything. But when Trick recognized Liberty, not a featured player but a star, he spotted the perfect subject for one of Boys Town's saddest con games. Blackie Norton informed Trick that there was money to be made from blackmailing closeted sports stars.

Trick forgot the gossip about Blackie Norton. His manipulative mind clicked into fast gear. He would have to pull off a coup. He would have to take Liberty to Blackie Norton.

———

Blackie Norton had decided to remain at the Bodycenter. He usually didn't spend more than an hour there. After all, time was money. But as Blackie was about to leave the shower, he spotted Paradise and Michael, arm in arm, entering the gym. Blackie was too smart to pay any attention, though he had been desperately in love with portraits of Paradise for years.

Michael represented the barrier to his lifelong dream. Paradise was obviously infatuated with the boy. Blackie Norton could understand the attraction. Youth. Blackie was rich, but there were certain things not even his wealth could buy. Somehow Blackie would find a way to ruin the relationship.

Blackie watched Paradise out of the corner of his eye while he toweled down in the gym. He did not watch Paradise undress. The other men, however, were excited over the possibilities of seeing the million-dollar, male-model strip show. They watched Paradise climb out of his gym shorts and place a jock strap around his perfect, muscle-rippling tanned torso.

Paradise was used to such attention and ignored the spectators. But when he spotted Blackie Norton certain familiar wheels began to churn in his brain. He knew Blackie's reputation and what Blackie could do for his career in Hollywood. One of the advantages of being a male beauty was using men in powerful positions.

Blackie Norton felt something stir in him that had been

dormant for years. By the time he had finished his conversation with Paradise in the locker room he decided to throw a gigantic, full-out party for Paradise and Michael. Very discreet, of course. He knew just how to make Paradise an offer he couldn't refuse. He rattled off the names of ten top Hollywood producers and at least twelve major stars who would be only too happy to help Paradise make it to the top of the heap in Hollywood. They didn't call Blackie the Gay Godfather because of his resemblance to Marlon Brando.

Blackie found Paradise enchanting. Much more innocent than Blackie would have believed. Blackie had not expected naivete and warmth from the Face of the Eighties. He not only wanted Paradise. He liked him. Blackie had always said that the beautiful boys of Boys Town were like race horses. They each had a season. Paradise was a thoroughbred. A classic. He would last.

Blackie took a trick pad, sheets of paper provided by the management for addresses and phone numbers of upcoming attractions, and gave Paradise the vital statistics. Sunday. They shook hands on it. Things were going quite well for Blackie Norton.

―――

Trick dialed Blackie Norton's private hot-line telephone number. The one used only for emergencies. Blackie was at home. He was *very* interested. Nothing satisfied Blackie Norton more than a juicy piece of hot gossip. Blackie instructed Trick to invite Liberty to the party for Paradise and Michael. His voice was calm and confident. Tell him not to worry. There would be women at the party to protect his reputation. Trick had dropped a time bomb in his lap. A sports star. This one might go down in the gay hall of fame.

7 BEL AIR – THE ROCK STAR

THE ROCK STAR WOKE ABOUT NOON. He had no idea what time it was. Barely remembered that he was in residence at his Bel Air estate, a $2.2-million villa modeled after William Randolph Hearst's San Simeon. He *was* aware that the residence dazzled his guests with its magnificent views of metropolitan El Lay and Catalina Island far away in the crayon-colored blue Pacific Ocean. For him, the hillside palace, a three-quarter-acre enclave, reminded him of the manner in which the aristocracy of England, his birthplace, had lived in the motion pictures of his childhood. So he bought it. Purchased the air of elegant sophistication. The richness of the fine woods, rare tiles, and marbles. The gourmet kitchen. The three spacious bedroom suites, each with its own bath, plus the 2600-square-foot master bedroom suite with its cherrywood paneled sitting room, a small kitchen, and a sumptuous bath.

To the amazement of his neighbors, an assortment of elegant Southern Californians who doted on golf scores and grappled with such problems as whether or not to serve grated onion with the caviar, he had installed a mammoth recreation center to the side of the immaculately kept landmark. The center, which included a gymnasium with a huge sauna and a lighted racquetball court, a separate brick pool house complete with a kitchen, and a large pool with an oversized spa, featured twenty-four-hour blaring rock-and-roll and an assortment of pleasure seekers, including wealthy sons and daughters of the international set, super-rich Arabs, El Lay's more elite dope dealers, a chorus line of socially prominent fashion models, as well as his own live-in girlfriend, a thirty-two-year-old platinum blonde movie starlet who was in charge of decoration and maintenance.

He hardly noticed the emerald green lawns, but they were extensive. Or the rose gardens. Or, in front of the mansion's main entrance, the white marble fountain with cherubs and lions' heads spouting water. The Rock Star hardly knew whether it was day or night.

The Rock Star did not care for quiet. He cranked up the music on his elaborate stereo system, sending choruses of chilling sounds throughout the mansion. A fleet of Rolls-Royces was already parked outside, dispatching guests who watched the servants repair the house from the ravages of the party the night before.

Bel Air? The Rock Star was aware of the fact that the few remaining blue bloods in residence considered it American society's foremost western outpost. But that was before dope. And high times. The aristocratic old guard, long dedicated to hard work, education, and the pursuit of perfection and truth, had been invaded by hordes of rock-and-roll barbarians who opened their ivy-walled playpens to processions of Bentleys, Jaguars, Mercedes-Benzes, and customized Jeeps filled with off-the-wall film directors, pipe-smoking porno princes, and the upper strata of the music business. On the surface Bel Air resembled the kind of community where residents struggled to even up taxes, improve their tennis, or keep up with the party circuit. But the show had changed. The old movie moguls were too incapacitated to fill their halls and salons and verandas with tinseled royalty in the 1980s. There were new people. Rod Stewart lived nearby. Alice Cooper somewhere up in the hills. Elton John and his entourage weren't far away. And a new style. The columnists called it Rock Riche. Never before in the history of the wealthy had people lived that way. Dressed that way. Moved that way. There had been something like Rock Riche in England during the sixties. But now Los Angeles had become God's Country. And long after midnight, society would toast a spectacular group of social wonders, most of whom were writing life off as a business expense.

The Rock Star had no idea how much the mansion cost. He read the price in the newspapers like everyone else. He could barely read. Never wrote at all — except his music. He asked his girlfriend to read him the stories in publications like *English Vogue* about his extravagant lifestyle. He had 3000 copies of comic books in the mansion. And 500 cases of Dom Perignon champagne. His fleet of cars numbered a Cadillac limousine, a Mercedes-Benz 450 SL, a Porsche Turbo, and two antique cars valued at over $1 million. He had grossed $20 million in 1980.

He was the most ordinary of men. There was nothing extraordinary about his facial features other than his trademark black hair, which looked as if it had been blown dry with egg beaters.

Before he became famous his thin, underfed body had never caused women or men palpitations. Yet he was an idol. A fixture in the world's dream life. A traditional ectomorph, but one with unparalleled wealth. Bel Air looked beautiful this morning. Suntanned beauty. God, he needed all he could get. He reached for the vial of cocaine on the Art Deco nightstand next to the 2000-year-old Gothic bed and snorted the rich adrenalin, awaiting its rocket-fuel blast of pleasure.

He never had to deal with what others referred to as the real world. Maids did his laundry. His girlfriend had little to do but shop the gilded, sumptuous boutiques of Los Angeles, surprising him daily with presents. His personal assistant tucked him in at night and in the morning dressed him in attire befitting his station in the social stratum of the world of rock-and-roll. Daily visitations to his estate by the rich and famous amused him at times. When he burst into tears under high-beamed ceilings in the living room or threw his frequent temper tantrums, demolishing thousands of dollars worth of antiques, the celebrated looked the other way. No one intended to rock the boat of a million-dollar star. He was a gold mine. He had been on the cover of *Rolling Stone* three times.

This was his first real day of rest in the last month. He had recently completed a thirty-day tour of twenty-seven cities in the United States. But the rush of life at the estate resembled the speed of a silent film classic. Since about twenty guests had already arrived, his personal assistant, a jolly former public relations man with enormous biceps and the motto, "Keep smiling," quickly dressed him in a finely tailored white suit imported from France. Then the Rock Star was rushed downstairs, through the grand hallway with its marble floors, to the kitchen for his daily breakfast of hot tea and croissants. Through a shrewd balance of uppers and downers he managed to enjoy the catatonic ecstasy of a parade of pamperers. First a masseur for a neck rub. Then a former gym instructor for his hair treatment. It didn't seem to matter who administered his pleasures — as long as his staff was composed of young men and women of incredible beauty. El Lay produced a bumper crop of free spirits. They never wore much. *That* felt like beauty.

    The woman who had brought him to the blue-skied, palm-treed paradise entered the kitchen. He felt a thrill. She, almost a decade older than he, was in a silky designer dress, and was trying to maintain a hold on youth with a stylish punk haircut. She was Belgian and had been married to an elegant movie star during a previous period of *La Dolce Vita* in Rome. Then her career faded. Being a companion to a rock star had once again given her status in Hollywood.

    The Rock Star had been intimate with many women. Almost anyone was available to him, from the Grade C groupies who hung out around the star-crossed nightclubs along the Sunset Strip to Grade B drones, secretaries, and publicists in the rich record companies to the A group, which consisted of almost everyone prominent in the movie-map world of El Lay.

    She, however, had provided him with class. When they walked into a chic restaurant the world of glamour sat by his side. All she had requested was extended credit at every store in Beverly Hills and a chance to organize the sit-down dinners for twenty-four she held once a week at the estate. In return, he turned her onto better drugs and unexpected sexual acts. It was the season for available, attractive women to be seen on the arms of flamboyant rock-and-roll *wunderkinder*. Alana Hamilton had divorced Gorgeous George to find her place in the sun with Rod Stewart. Bianca Jagger had traded in her Nicaraguan pedigree to marry and then divorce Mick Jagger. Cher had switched from Sonny to Gregg Allman to Gene Simmons. The Rock Star's woman clearly didn't like him — but she loved him. At these prices, with the world so economically unstable, he obviously presented the greatest hedge against inflation for a beautiful woman. No one reached the levels of wealth of a rock star anymore, or journeyed to such forbidden extremes. He watched her depart with a girlfriend to go shopping. He smoked his first joint of the day, allowing the music and rich dope to invade his brainwaves. It was going to be a good day. But then, for a long time, there hadn't been a bad one.

His reverie was interupted by a phone call. Normally he wouldn't have bothered, but it was his lawyer. An ex-girlfriend, a former playmate who had burned out in the overindulgent stream of things, was publishing a book detailing her days and nights with him. He was pissed. But that was rock-and-roll. He turned the music up louder. Threw his hair back and let himself slip into the fantasy world of his high and his music. Everyone was arriving to glimpse a star. Today they would. He felt wild. El Lay was just beginning to happen. Since it was so far from everywhere else it had pioneered new ways of pleasure. Today he would have it all. He breathed in the wealth surrounding him, let out a howl, and prepared for total wildness. Nobody did it better. When he felt good, he danced around the room. Today he was going to dance. He may not have been a woman's dream. But he was exotic. There was a big demand for such a specimen.

The guests were already cavorting in the den, a wonderful old baronial, high-ceilinged room with a huge fireplace and decorated to give the impression of the interior of an English king's court. The room smelled of fresh-cut flowers. When the Rock Star entered all action stopped. All attention focused on his every move. For many of the guests this was a new show. They had seen the movie stars. The movie producers. The rich European aristocrats. But a rock star was something fresh to include in their personal journals. They were agonizingly aware of the easy money in this area and convinced that it could be theirs for a few right words.

If they felt like having a drink, two butlers were at their beck and call. The maids served them dope on silver trays. Fifty-dollar-a-bottle champagne flowed. The music? Only the best. It was Christmas, New Year's, Halloween every hour. A national holiday had been declared.

If they were lucky that day, or beautiful, or famous — or all of the above — they might be treated to a personal tour of the estate. With the Rock Star by their side, they would step through secret passageways, sink into thick, white carpets, and enter rooms dominated by elaborate electronics and medieval suits of armor. If you wanted something to eat, food was provided instantly. If the weather was good, why not a swim?

The afternoons were filled with play. What the Rock Star was inclined to refer to as "recess." Frisbee on the lawns. Skateboarding on the immaculate driveways in front of the electronically controlled gates. Croquet in the gardens, if that was your thing. The fact that many of the players in the informal volleyball championships were paid $150 a day for the pleasure of their company was not discussed. The Rock Star collected people. Many of them were common variety hangers-on, a breed of hairdressers on dangerous drugs and water-ski instructors picked up at luxurious resorts in the Caribbean. They lasted only until their initial passion for the mile-a-minute world of rock-and-roll was drained by the high-sensation daily barrage of dope and sport. One morning they would wake up after having passed out on the carpeting the night before and suddenly the strange things happening around them weren't funny anymore. You never saw much of them after that.

Those who lasted were more enamored of the rock-and-roll magic carpet ride. They understood that the days and nights in Bel Air were simply brief respites from the real role of the Rock Star. They were aware of a human wall around the Rock Star, preventing any anxiety or stress from appearing in the subterranean recesses of his personality. There was no strain to stardom. Performing was a cinch. Once the Rock Star went on stage he got a hit off his power. He could turn 18,000 people in Shea Stadium or Madison Square Garden into instant lovers. Grab audiences up in his hands, and at the right minute release the ecstasy and frenzy that brought them to worship his talent. But there was a torturous price to pay. The machinery of the rock world never ground to a halt. The Rock Star was required to keep one step ahead of his public, stay on schedule, remain on tour, get the next album out, do the promotion. It went on forever. There were no days off. He must work twenty-four hours a day to stay on top. Once he interrupted the flow, he could be finished forever.

It was like living in a bubble. He needed an entourage to shield him from the constant criticism. To pump up his image. Anyone who wasn't willing to play the game was removed within minutes from his presence by security guards, trained like police dogs to sniff out disloyalty.

The Rock Star had given up trying to fathom all of the things that had happened to him in the past year. In the last month. In that day alone. He no longer cared how incapacitated he was, because everything was done for him. They treated him like an infant. So he began to act like one. His life, his daily existence was only part of a grand eighty-mile-an-hour plan drawn up in an agent's office on the Sunset Strip. All that mattered really was that he paid off. He was doing that royally.

By 3 P.M. lunch had arrived. Somebody, one of the fresh young hopeless or famous things who arrived daily, had gone down to the city and brought back marvelous munchies from the Rock Star's favorite junk-food hamburger chain, Jack in the Box. Hamburgers, cheeseburgers, malts, onion rings, french fries, and sugar-spreckled popover pies. The music was turned up to its maximum level. Party hats and streamers were brought into the den. A groupie, a movie starlet who had just completed a cameo in *Flash Gordon,* with green polish on her toenails and a poinsettia tucked behind her blonde fairy-tale coiffure, had purchased 600 darts and thirty-two guns from a toy store. Valiums and Quaaludes were passed around with the champagne. The cooks had prepared a rich chocolate mousse cake, decorating it like a birthday surprise.

By four, the servants had lit the fireplace and the Rock Star's girlfriend had returned from her shopping spree. She was on a suspender kick. Her arrival was a signal for the others to disappear politely into the outer spaces of the estate. Her perfume filled the room. Her soft voice carried the grace of a born actress. There could be no doubt that she was beautiful. The Rock Star took her in his arms.

Only her intimates knew that she was one of the world's better masseuses. She undressed the Rock Star, placed him on his stomach, and from a mantelpiece selected an aromatic oil, applying it to his back. Her strokes were firm, confident, and she was familiar with all the pressure points. The back of his neck. The spinal muscles near the curvature of the waist. The muscles of his arms. The massage was slow and warm and peaceful. He loved the way she pulled and stroked his buttocks and the calves of his legs.

When she started on his feet he growled with pleasure. She kneaded the foot muscles with trained expertise, and when she was finished he asked for more. Turning him over, she expertly massaged his chest, pausing to caress his nipples. Her strong hands found his ribs and worked each of them into relaxation, toured his stomach, and whisked through his pubic hair. She knew exactly what he desired but continually surprised him with unexpected turns of the hand. She had trained him to communicate verbally during sexual passion. Her European background had encouraged few sexual hang-ups. Her hands rummaged through his thick hair as she fingered his scalp, all the time moving her own body to the music pouring into the luxuriantly upholstered room. She may not have been a film star anymore. But on the casting couches with the world's richest men she was still a contender. The Rock Star removed her clothing and caressed her voluptuous body.

The woman was aware that the Rock Star had moped about El Lay for years, observing the rock renaissance, sampling California sexuality, and absorbing the mannerisms of the world of rock-and-roll. It had paid off. He had become one of the publicized men of the times. Anyone seen with him became a candidate for notoriety. They wanted to touch the woman who touched the Rock Star. In the music world, as she appraised it, there were only stars. Everyone else was a groupie. She had seen the biggest producers in the business cross the steamy and smoky rock hangouts in New York to strangle hold a star like Mick Jagger. The fact that her lifestyle produced an open-house policy for every offbeat character who passed through Hollywood only added to her own legend.

She had witnessed impromptu duets between the Rock Star and Elton John. Held him tight after an ex-girlfriend had threatened to seek revenge by casting voodoo spells on the front lawn. It *was* romantic. A dizzying ride along the edges of stardom. She gave herself to him. It was all ephemeral anyway. She was enjoying herself immensely. He paid her $5000 a week.

When the pleasure was over, the Rock Star was not sated. The girlfriend left to prepare dinner and to take her daily siesta in the bedroom far from the brutal sunshine. But he was not sleepy. He needed only a bath and a change to go on for hours. The Rock Star could get excited over anything, though it never seemed to last more than seven minutes.

On the last tour every city he visited seemed to be striving for total depravity. Every teenager burdened with possessions. He met sixteen-year-olds with their own Rolls-Royces and drivers in many of the cities. The public was fascinated with his wealth and how he spent it. That was why people loved him, and why they ripped him off.

As he examined the huge hulk of a house, he mulled over the next tour, one of many to Japan. The logistics alone were staggering. The tentative crew, all hand-picked by him, included ten members of the band, a tour director, an advance man, a six-member road crew, ten members for stage production, a master electrician, a master carpenter, eight technicians, six truck drivers, and three singers for the opening act.

His own plane, a huge DC-10, was being prepared. Most of the seats had been replaced with pillows at his request. There were rumors that the two stewardesses had been dismissed from commercial airlines on morality charges, but it wasn't true. It must have been some other rock act.

On top of that, the music industry was in financial trouble. Many of the old acts were fading away, unable to draw the big crowds of a more prosperous era. To win in the rock game these days, you had to stage incredible productions that required mammoth sets.

One false step, and you were stranded in some hick town for the rest of your life. Somebody had to make sure that the bus company and the limousine service were on their way. Check weather conditions here and in the next tour town. Confirm the newspaper, TV, and magazine interviews and place hotel room keys in separate envelopes, which also included detailed room lists. Each day there was a manager simply to count names and make sure that each band member boarded the plane in time to perform on schedule. The monotony of it all was hideous. The repetition. The waiting. But they were all earning unbelievable amounts of money and traveling first class, in some cases for the first time in their lives. Sleeping in posh suites. Residing at the best hotels. Slugging only the choicest of the paparazzi. Elvis had done it. The Beatles had done it. It was politely called paying your dues.

The California moon was out now, huge and golden over the Pacific. The gardens outside fragrant with honeysuckle. New guests were arriving. The Rock Star could hear their hysterical laughter filling the rooms of the house. He decided on a game of pool. The game room was furnished with a pool table, pinball and Ping-Pong machines. Children loved it. So did the Rock Star. He wasn't a fabulous pool player, but then he was fabulous at other things.

Guests of a more literate bent were often surprised at the conversations in the pool room. It was as if a group of basketball or football players were discussing game strategy. Dazzled by the wealth of the setting and the elegance of the estate, one might have expected cocktail chatter. The Rock Star, however, never said much. When he wasn't incoherent or sullen, he spent most of his time embracing the nubile, Spandex-covered young women in the room. They looked surprisingly like the Rock Star. The others, younger rock-and-roll addicts and older men in fine Cardin suits who had forsaken the garment industry to produce records on the Sunset Strip in floor-to-ceiling carpeted suites, were highly drugged. They were discussing a recent casualty in the rock world. A thirty-five-year-old legend who had O.D.'d the night before in Cincinnati. He had become too old to tour, they commented, as casually as most people discuss the weather conditions. But the age crisis in the rock world was all too true. The new kids in town kept getting younger each year. Sometimes you couldn't stick around waiting for your style to come back into vogue, like the Beach Boys. Often it didn't. In the tough world of rock-and-roll, you were only as good as your current position on the *Billboard* charts. Tomorrow depended on what happened at the cash registers in the record shops. There was nothing worse than being an old rock star.

The Rock Star reached for escape. The underground dope circles in Los Angeles were always creating a new high. The latest was a form of super-speed known as Crank. He took one of the small, white pills from a twenty-four-karat-gold Tiffany case, popped it into his mouth, and drowned his throat with champagne. He didn't hurt physically. But inside. He examined the group in front of him, lost in conversation and in game playing. If he had any compassion, he would send most of them to the highly paid doctors in Beverly Hills. The stress and strain — the drinking and the dope — had taken their toll. Underneath the glamour, there was fatigue. But *they* could afford a few days in the rich spas of California, the ones with the fancy Mexican names reaping fortunes from the manic-depressives in the music business. The Rock Star didn't have time. The cultured few who visited his world never returned. They declared him an asshole and shifted their attention to people less rich but much less tortured.

He didn't care about them anyway. There were always friends around. Friends sensitive to the Rock Star's unexpressed wishes and to his Heathcliffian moods. They came along for the ride, for the festive luncheons, and sat for hours in zombie-like trances watching TV monitors offering the minor tragedies of "General Hospital" and "As the World Turns" and the antics of contestants on "Family Feud" and "Password Plus" — the Rock Star's favorite programs.

Around ten it was agreed by mutual consent to go out for dinner. Five years ago you either stayed home or dined at the funky Mexican restaurants in El Lay or ate by candlelight or incense sticks at health-food parlors operated by brotherhoods and religious cults which grew their organic produce in retreats in the hills of Topanga Canyon.

The rise of Rock Riche in El Lay had brought into existence a group of European and New York record tycoons with pleasures and tastes far beyond the comprehensions of the sleepy, kicked-back natives. By 1981, from Malibu to Hollywood, a string of haute cuisine palaces, all incredibly lavish and built at costs in the millions, had blown in from nowhere, like summer winds, to feed the new worlds of fast wealth.

By eleven, the Rock Star and "the family" had arrived at Le Dome, a Sunset Strip French restaurant which had Corinthian columns on the outside and rich green velvet dining rooms inside. Le Dome was filled most nights with record producers, rock stars, managers, groupies, publicists, and the entire rainbow of drug dealers and con artists who appeared wherever rock-and-rollers gathered. Le Dome provided a setting and an ambience for the rock world to meet and make deals.

The Rock Star understood the restaurant business from years of study. Le Dome survived off celebrity. The owners, two Frenchmen supported by "secret" investors, were expected by their clientele to provide more than the atmosphere of a chic Parisian brasserie. El Lay diners were hungry for status, not cuisine.

The group was quickly ushered to their seats, in a private dining room in the back of the restaurant, beyond the climbers' front-seat sanctuaries, and immediately stroked by the maitre d's. There had already been a request from a French journal for a photograph; request denied. The Rock Star was heavily inebriated, but he wasn't dumb. He never allowed a photograph, not even a candid, unless he had a makeup artist on hand. It brought him confidence. Besides, stars who got high on coke and speed got very funny in front of a camera. He had learned from experience that his eyes barely existed in the actual photograph. But he gave the maitre d' his publicist's name and told him to relay it to the photographer.

He had been trained never to alienate the press — unless it was good for the story. The more people who knew your name, the farther you rose in the world of rock. He hadn't been as successful in the publicity game as others. He neither spouted the left-wing causes, which appealed to the editors of the rock magazines, nor was he bisexual. But he could fall into a pool as well as the next rock star. Kick ass in an auto race. His girlfriend *was* a movie star. The editors didn't consider him sexy, or photograph him because he looked great, but reporters earned their living drumming up stories and photos. Eccentrics were currently fashionable.

Dinner was served. Since the Rock Star was not a culinary critic, and many of his guests had trouble deciphering the French menu, the owners had selected the meal and hoped their fine china would not end up as souvenirs in the handbags of the entourage.

First, the elegantly prepared hors d'oeuvres, including escargots, the traditional French delicacy cooked in garlic, butter, and Pernod sauce; Scampi aux Fines Herbes (large shrimp lightly sautéed in garlic butter and fine herbs); Saumon Fumé (delicately smoked salmon, complemented with watercress, mushrooms, capers, and onion) and Tarte aux Oignons (a fabulous quiche prepared with onions). The wine waiters served fine wines until the main courses arrived. Steak tartare for the Rock Star. He was constantly watching his waistline. The others chose from a filet of sole adorned with walnuts and vegetables, a plate of firm breasts of chicken served with lemon wedges, and a Pacific snapper entree flavored with lemon and capers. By the time the crème caramels and peach melbas and the requisite birthday layer cake arrived (it was not the Rock Star's birthday, but it was a trademark) the group was in high spirits.

The Rock Star stared at the scene through the picture windows behind the group and took in the romantic mural of the extravagantly neon-lit city below Le Dome. The winds and the tropical rains had blown the pollution away and the city was starkly, monumentally beautiful. The moonlight outlining its hills and valleys and oceansides. He had everything. Wealth. Position. Power. The estate in Bel Air. The elegant girlfriend. Hundreds of friends. The Grammys. The clothes. The celebrity. One of the entourage raised his glass in a general toast. "To the Rock Star," he said. "Long live the King."

Since he was on good speaking terms with his liver, he

drank and welcomed the cheers, the applause. He took the birthday cake in his fingers and ate it like a truck driver in a roadside diner. More applause. The after-dinner snort of cocaine. He lifted his own glass for his own toast.

"You are not your results," he said.

The mixture of coke and speed sent the room whirling. He could hear the conversations around the table at Le Dome. Full of bitchy rock-and-roll stories. Comments about the latest rock-and-roller bent on self-destruction. He heard one of his own songs thunder from the sound system at the restaurant. Felt the stares of the crowd observing him in public. He passed out, his egg-beater haircut and his famous face — the face adored by millions, the subject of numerous billboards on the drive-in art gallery that was the Sunset Strip — falling into the birthday cake.

He was twenty-five years old.

8 THE RESTAURANT

1 P.M., BEVERLY HILLS

"Heennry daarrlliiing!"
A woman, fortyish, blonde, her hair pressed back into a sleek chignon, her silk blouse and skirt ruffling in the wind, moves exquisitely towards Henry Berger's table one sunspreckled afternoon at Ma Maison. She was Berger's type of woman. Not a movie star patched together to resemble her fading screen image by the plastic surgeon patrols of Beverly Hills. But a woman whom the Greek Chorus at the Hollywood hangout to end all hangouts would refer to as a Beverly Hills Green Goddess. A wealthy woman. A woman of means. A woman who preferred the creature comforts. Perhaps a slight bit too uptight by current fashion — though ready to loosen at least two buttons on her carob-colored shirt. The woman had fine hands. That was important, because in Berger's *Screen Stories* view of life women should have fine hands. Beautifully groomed. Smelling of Chloe perfume with the scent of Parisian artistry about it.

An extraordinary moment. Berger's eyes meet hers. Her eyes meet Berger's. There is an air of flirtation to the whole scene. Liz Smith, the New York gossip columnist in residence in Hollywood that week, glances up from her salade Niçoise and makes a mental note. Now if Henry married again, thought Liz, that would be news. Liz Smith didn't look as if she peeped under beds and tallied up legendary couplings for a living. She had the appearance of a benevolent librarian. Very Julia Child. Very New York class and all that. "Somebody ought to give her a joint and mellow her out," said a movieland banker with curly surfer hair who wore a benign, blissed-out expression through most of his working hours. Still, that was the reason anyone in their right mind went to Ma Maison. To be seen. To be recorded. It was practically the only place in town where a reservation guaranteed you a front-row seat to watch the Hollywood elite at play. It was important.

Henry Berger was a living relic of Beverly Hills. An endangered species. He was Old Hollywood stayin' alive in New Hollywood. Big buck rock-'n-rollers scrambling for center seats at the fashionable show-biz restaurants in Beverly Hills would smoke a funny cigarette in their Rolls-Royce and then barrel into laid-back, four-star playpens like Ma Maison, look at Berger, and laugh. My God, the guy *was* a character. He looked as if he had been rented from the 1940s rack at Western Costume. Did anyone use a black Dunhill cigarette holder with a gold tip anymore? Berger, the last of the Hollywood romantics, did. Was anyone outside of the late, late show seen wearing his hair combed back and sprayed with water like Franchot Tone? Berger was. Jesus, Hollywood had changed. The Gabor sisters were wearing jeans, for God's sake. Yet Berger spoke with a bedroom baritone like Charles Boyer's. Young punks and Elvis Presley return-alikes with amazing blood-curdling red hair were strutting the studio lots like earringed roosters inspecting a henhouse. Berger went for his manicure to the Pink Palace — the Beverly Hills Hotel. The latest society thing — the absolute *latest* — was Disco Roller-Skating. Very "Charlie's Angels." Berger preferred Bobby Short.

His tailored sports coats — tweedy and English, made for him by his own tailor in Manhattan — belonged to the Fred Astaire–Ginger Rogers era. The gold Gucci bracelet dangling from his okay-but-not-great tanned right wrist (a gift from a Berger follower, he said) was, well, to put it bluntly, sugar-daddy time. Yet, everyone stared. Some even came over to offer the ultimate status overture — the famous Hollywood "kiss, kiss" which, if executed properly, never, no *never*, allowed the kisser's lips to graze the smoothly shaved visage of the kissee. Berger was somewhere between fifty-four and heaven, and his midsection was sadly in need of a tummy tuck. Still, an amazing sight. Something like seeing a living Hollywood museum porcelain piece. What the stargazers — who noticed Berger lunch after lunch at the Golden Troika of show-biz bistros, Ma Maison, the Polo Lounge of the Beverly Hills Hotel (they serve pink salad dressing), and the star-packed Bistro Garden in Beverly Hills — wondered was, Who *was* that man who looked like Franklin Delano Roosevelt and seemed, well, like somebody?

Berger didn't work. He had made his money off Cricket cigarette lighters. He had never starred in a movie, not even a bit part. And yet Berger wound himself up every day like a Cary Grant doll and worked his way very nicely through endless lunches, dinners, and elegant parties. What most people do for a lark — dress up and drink, dine, dance, and make love to the rich and famous — occupied Berger twenty-four hours a day. He was a professional Beverly Hills partygoer machine.

The bitchy set at Ma Maison dubbed Berger, who had

been married to the late Anita Louise, as *the* geriatric escort service — a man who still opened limousine doors for his dates, sent red roses with a card, and treated women as if they were perpetually wearing Chanel No. 5. Definitely presexual liberation. The movieland social yentas claimed that Berger had played the dating game with, well, *everyone*. Rita Hayworth? Oh, yes! She had starred in *Gilda*, and there wasn't anyone in Fantasyland today with Rita's kind of hot cha-cha glamour. Or money. No wonder Berger haunts old legends the way real estate salesmen search for mansions. Berger has escorted Lana Turner, Ann Miller, Jane Russell, Shirley Jones, Gloria de Haven, Linda Christian, Barbara Stanwyck, and even Loretta Young.

"Heenry Daarrling!"

Ma Maison, as Berger well knew, wasn't a restaurant at all — but a nonstop private party. It had changed the fashion in Hollywood in more ways than one, Berger thought. In the Golden Days of the city — the period in which Berger was trained like a samurai to live the life of the Old Hollywood exquisite man about town — the town thrived on restaurants like Chasen's and the Bistro. These places practiced classic ego-massage and "A" table routine that fit a period in the town's history when stars wore gowns and their dates wore white dinner jackets. You went respectable. But six years ago a mysterious Frenchman by the name of Patrick Terrail — Berger, because of his cachet, simply called him Patrick — had managed to create a new taste and at the same time turn an old, dilapidated Hollywood bungalow in one of the less prestigious sections of the city — Melrose Avenue — into a new center of fashion and fine dining. Ma Maison didn't look like much, not unless you snapped a quick shot of the twenty-two gray Rolls-Royces that usually lined its driveways at all important lunch hours. (And that meant every day, because Terrail hand-picked his luncheon and dinner guest lists like French Revolutionaries prepared for a hanging.) Ma Maison had an open-air patio for dining, crummy Astroturf carpets. Charming, but not that expensive. White tables. A staff of black-and-white-costumed waiters who, as many pointed out, weren't that hunky and certainly didn't have the dignity of the old days. And a troop of Mexican and Central American illiterate bus boys whose favorite expression upon being paged by one of the dandyish regulars turned out to be, "No speek Inglesa." Well, it *was* Beverly Hills. And it *was* sunny. And a great place to show off a tan. And everyone was into ecology. So the idea of a small French country restaurant where the regulars comprised the crème de la crème of the covers of *People* magazine sounded marvelous.

Nobody who came to Ma Maison remained blasé. Some were anxious, even terrified of committing a faux pas in such an atmosphere. They soon discovered that nobody was watching them. The eyes of the Hollywood Greek Chorus — those, like Berger, who had nothing to do all day but spend two or three hours at their immaculate toilette or read about who was plucking whom in the trade papers, *Daily Variety* and the *Hollywood Reporter* — were always on the central platform. There Terrail, who *was* a power in the town — a prince of the restaurant scene of High Hollywood — would receive his guests, and if they were stars spend a moment doing a shtick with them so that guests could get some free entertainment with their fresh green beans with goose liver paté. You could overlook your dues to the Screen Actors Guild, the chorus chanted, but you *never* did not pay your bill at Ma Maison.

To Berger Ma Maison was a sublime combination of the Golden Days of Hollywood and the High Hollywood new breed. The French restaurant had become so legendary that a low-rent copy, the Moustache Café, had opened a couple of blocks down the road. Berger realized that the people who frequented Moustache were merely training for the big time. And the big time was Ma Maison. If a restaurant could represent a talk show or an Oscar telecast, then Ma Maison was that restaurant for High Hollywood. The place was so exclusive that its telephone number was unlisted.

Wasn't that Margaret Trudeau over in a corner, looking lovely and slightly anxious doing a Garbo number? Didn't Bianca Jagger, the glamorous ex-wife of rock singer Mick, just come down the platform after pausing for her star moment, which allowed each new performer at Ma Maison to take a bow and sign in please?

Terrail wore $800 European designer suits some days and rather glorified California laid-back work shirts and denims on others. He could often get quite snooty. Terrail knew all the latest gossip on everyone. Yet when you got to know him — having spent a great deal of money at Ma Maison to prove your dedication to his whimsical rituals — Terrail was cool. He often placed Band-Aids over blouses on ladies whose see-through nipples were obviously scandalous and things like that. After all, he wasn't just another restaurant owner. He arranged the whole lunchtime show at Ma Maison like a major studio production. It wasn't exactly Rick's Café Americaine from *Casablanca,* Berger thought. But close. Close.

Who were the Ma Maison regulars? A mix of newspaper and television columnists, movie producers, movie stars, overnight television sensations, public relations experts, and fashionable establishment types who would boycott their favorite spot if they found out that their daily production was becoming polluted by people from ... God forbid, Encino! Terrail never disappointed his audience. Each day he directed about 100 myth makers into his patio and presided over the festivities like one of those old-time radio announcers going berserk at a movie premiere.

Berger was more than a regular. He was an unofficial club member. It wasn't totally Berger's scene, in fact, for he quietly turned his elegant back on the dressed-to-kill dope dealers and the rattily attired rock stars. At least once a week and often twice Berger would stride into the celebrity sea, taking a seat at his favorite table, lighting a Chesterfield (none of these filters for Berger baby; they reminded him of a junior Tampax or something) in his gold-tipped cigarette holder, and ceremoniously displaying his hand-tailored finery. Ah, yes, Berger would say, it wasn't Proustian, that was for sure. But Ma Maison *was* fun. A wonderful, star-studded fashion show. So elegant and yet so kicked back. Yes. Exactly.

Click! Cheryl Tiegs, the blonde, tallish cover girl and TV commentator — God, wasn't it scandalous how she left her husband for that *photographer* — entered Ma Maison like a blast of High Hollywood perfume. Not exactly Liz Taylor, mind you, but she had all those qualities that fans earning $200 a week, receiving $10-a-year raises, and finding life either low, lower, or lowest wanted to get high on. Blonde hair so squeaky clean and full that it craved a camera. Teeth so white she could have posed for the Master Race. Wasn't that what Ma Maison was all about? The vicarious thrill of mixing with myths? Take that fork out of your spinach salad and gawk!

Click! Kitty Tanen, the wife of one of Universal's head honchos, entered. Conversation levels died for a moment, diners took in her full-length, elegant, dark beauty, well-dressed for the occasion by Parisian loony-tunes designer Karl Lagerfeld (they say he looks like Dracula, darling) and watched as Tanen moved like a Renaissance princess to her freshly painted white wooden throne.

Click! Suzanne Pleshette arrives. Oh, my God, she's in

those denim overalls again. But Suzanne, dear girl, can carry it off. Look how she shows that dazzling smile. Look how Terrail takes her denim conductor's cap off her TV head — the same head you've seen on all those Bob Newhart TV shows — and is having fun with Suzanne. Old shtick, really. But then think how much fun it will be to tell everyone tonight that you saw Suzanne and she is still kicking up her tennis shoes? Is she wearing a bra? Find out.

Click! Freddie Fields, the gregarious producer of such epics as *Looking for Mr. Goodbar*, enters. *Who* could stand the ending, but then nobody is ever happy anymore on the screen, are they? He makes a dignified entrance, smiles at the throng, and shakes hands with the high and the mighty as his party moves to a central table. Do you think Freddie might be interested in that novel about the Revolutionary War I read last night? It was pretty sexy. *Maybe* he would go for it?

Click! Click! Nina Van Pallandt. She was involved in that Clifford Irving forgery scandal and appears in all those Robert Altman pictures like *A Wedding* — she played a bitch, didn't she? — and almost rates applause. Okay, Nina, show off that Scandinavian porcelain face. Okay, Nina, shake those bootees inside that $800 Charles Gallay frock. Oooh, Nina, where did you get those shoes? Marvelous, darling, divine.

Click! The Gabor family enters en masse, including Mama Gabor flanked on the right by the well-fed Zsa Zsa, and on the left by the beaming Eva. Now, this is what we came for! God, hasn't Zsa Zsa put on weight? She looks like she's trying to grab the spotlight from town heavyweight Shelley Winters. Her new marriage to that lawyer, what's his name? — her seventh, isn't it? — must agree with her. And Eva, well, she's a dear, but she's got to stop walking around Beverly Hills dressed like Marie Antoinette. Mama can hardly walk! But she looks wonderful. They all do. I mean, legends. Do you suppose those jewels are real? Probably paste. Because those Gabors are smart underneath all that cotton-candy hair. God, what a scene!

When the Greek Chorus of Hollywood has finished with the Gabors they return to their cuisine, which for El Lay is considered not bad.

Berger orders another white wine. He has long since retired from going to the movies. All the theaters show is *Star Wars* (which he hasn't seen) and science fiction dreck. Ma Maison, on the other hand, features the movie magic of his generation. The ultimate drawing room comedy. With loads of gossip (had he heard, for example, the latest about Barbra Streisand? Well, it seems the Queen of Lotus-Land was firing people right and left. Streisand, according to the Ma Maison crowd, would enter a set, smile at a few people, and immediately have them thrown off the lot. She didn't like their auras or something). Berger didn't care about alienation movies or teenage gang pictures. What he relished were rich, aimless people celebrating their success by going to Ma Maison. Ma Maison was now part of the entertainment history books. First your portrait in *Variety*, next a shopping spree at the endless Beverly Hills boutiques, and then a celebrity lunch at Ma Maison.

At one time or another you could spot Orson Welles, Jack Lemmon, Michael Caine, and founder Gene Kelly breaking croissants there. Or Jack Jones, Donald Sutherland, Jacqueline Bisset, Marisa Berenson, and rock star Boz Scaggs having six out of ten meals there. But Berger looked beyond the stars to the real power elite — the money men who headed what was left of the major studios. He spotted Dennis Stanfill, the man behind Twentieth-Century-Fox.

He ate at Ma Maison practically every day. Paramount Pictures head Barry Diller, MGM's David Begelman, along with movie mogul Kirk Kerkorian. And wasn't that Dino De Laurentiis talking a deal with French director Louis Malle, who did *Pretty Baby*? Yes, deals were made at Ma Maison. And careers ruined by the improper use of a fork.

It didn't take much to break into the whole Hollywood social scene; Berger was aware of that. Any young man — Berger called the species Morning Glories — could arrive at the doors of Ma Maison and enter into the endless rounds of parties and gossip and beautiful girls for say, $20,000 to $30,000. That could last six months if the young man were shrewd and dressed as if he had just stepped out of *Gentlemen's Quarterly*. All it took to look successful in Beverly Hills was a small down payment on a mansion, a leased Mercedes-Benz (preferably gray), and an idea to sell to a movie producer. Even if you didn't make it, you had enjoyed the whole Beverly Hills experience — the nude swims at Hugh Hefner's, the elegant dinners at super-agent Swifty Lazar's, the movie premieres. And it only cost you what it might cost to go around the world. That was Hollywood, Berger said. It was like Las Vegas — people turned over like card dealers.

The only difference between Ma Maison and a fancy restaurant anywhere else was the fact that you got to practice invasion of privacy. Oh yes, said Berger, still recovering from some fancy party the night before and speaking in a voice that sounded like too many cigarettes and much too much champagne, every town had its Ma Maison. But it wasn't the same. Because Hollywood was the Olympus of America. The whole world eagerly awaited stories about the comings and goings of celebrities. And the deals weren't just one-liners. They made headlines in the columns across the movieland network. If John Travolta signed for a $3-million deal at Ma Maison, people *wanted* to read about it. The new breed had tried to bulldoze Berger's brand of Hollywood. They had taken away the beautiful, dressy clubs on the Strip, like Ciro's and Mocambo's, replacing them with toned-down backgammon joints like Pipp's and strange, frantic private discos like Club Elysée. But as long as the public longed for royalty there would be places and scenes like Ma Maison. Berger congratulated himself on the good luck to have a front-row seat at the trash and tears of High Hollywood. Each day he lived for those extraordinary moments when he could brush elbows with the untouchables of the American dream. Henry looked up from his table and smiled. They weren't making Henry Berger movies anymore. So Berger just invented his own.

9 THE FAD

From out of nowhere, it seemed, roller-skating had become The Craze in California. Joggers were passé. So what if they had rediscovered every grassy strip from Eureka to San Diego? Once you'd done one 10-K run, you'd done them all. Surfing? Well, everyone knows what happened to surfing. Gidget was middle-aged, for God's sake. Cycling still had some glory to it. But those strange costumes — black-and-white-striped uniforms, combined with tanned limbs — made devotees of the sport look like creatures in an old Mack Sennett silent comedy. They were all pastimes — like strobe lights and disco dancing — which everyone in trend-conscious California had long since crossed off their Hermès appointment schedules. Disco decadents with their veils and their flame-retardant Snow White princess costumes and Joan Crawford fuck-me high-heeled shoes were as out of style as hippies in 1980s California.

Then this roller-skating fad happened. Wheels of grape and lavender and rainbow colors. People of such impeccable golden breeding that they could have been ads from a catalog of the California good life. Almost everyone was trying it — politicians to win elections, movie star luminaries, sports champions, labor leaders, millionaire industrialists, Socially Registered Easterners, and even royalty. A new bliss machine on wheels. It was all the rage.

Wealthy tourists — the kind of people who had done Disneyland and Magic Mountain and lolled in their $700-a-day private penthouses at the exclusive L'Ermitage Hotel — would be tooling down La Cienega Boulevard in Hollywood and stopping at the red light at Santa Monica Boulevard. Suddenly their eyes would bug out as if they'd seen a really extraordinary sight. A vision. In front of them stood this old refurbished 1950s-style bowling alley freshly painted in thick lavender and blazing with neon lights like the marquees outside Broadway theaters blaring: FLIPPER'S ROLLER BOOGIE PALACE.

By day, Flipper's was a hangout for rich teenagers. Celebrities took their kids down for a few twirls around the track. Mon Dieu, a tourist type from Paris was yelling right in the middle of Flipper's, isn't that Jim Brown, the former football star and actor out on the track with his daughter? Doesn't he look, well, sexy, in those cut-off red shorts and that white, white T-shirt atop his massive, athletic frame? Stars on wheels? What could they say back on the Champs-Elysées?

At night, Flipper's is transformed into the Studio 54 on wheels of High Hollywood. On Monday night you could watch rock star Elton John out on the rink. John, in an incredibly lizardy, space-age green jumpsuit was flying by at speeds that seemed to break the sound barrier. And 500 other skaters in equally outrageous gear were barreling down the track following John, inspecting his latest hair transplant.

Thursday was Rock-'n-Roll Night. Wasn't that Suzanne Somers standing in the middle of the rink between the four listless, plastic palm trees which looked as if they'd been bathed in moonlight dust? Green must have been the color this year. Suzanne, with her blonde, get-me-back-to-Marilyn-Monroe hair and her eat-your-heart-out-Farrah-Fawcett voluptuous body stood regally while photographers from all the social gazettes flashed away at yet another big star going the roller-skate route.

Margaux Hemingway, the model and Ernest Hemingway's granddaughter, had attended Flipper's. Matt Collins, the million-dollar-smile male model and the cover boy of *Looking Good*, did backflips over the lavish landmark. Régine, the flaming red-haired goddess of the Jet Set disco clubs, even filmed her French television special from the sports palace.

New Yawkers who were visiting California to collect a few new jokes were entranced. Flipper's wasn't some resurrected dilapidated roller-skating rink in Brooklyn with piped-in disco music. It wasn't the Reseda Roller Rink over the hill in the San Fernando Valley, the hall which Cher had discovered and brought to the attention of the cutting-edge people a few years ago.

Flipper's was America's top citadel of roller chic. It was more than a skating rink. It was a full-fledged Southern California fantasy. A modern-day pleasure palace with all the innocence and beauty of a Disney animated full-length feature. For one thing, the track itself was huge, painted to resemble the yellow brick road Dorothy skipped down in *The Wizard of Oz*. For another, the Hollywood High Tech rafters were filled with pink and blue lights, which bathed the skaters in an ethereal light show. Flipper's reeked of class. Luxuriously upholstered banquettes surrounded the rink. Above the banquettes were richly paneled V.I.P. lounges where the roller elite dined and drank and engaged in a spectator sport which most considered worth the hefty $500 yearly private membership fee. Designer-dressed cocktail waitresses skated nonchalantly to your Masonite table. It was strictly top skate.

There had always been golfing and tennis clubs for the social set in Hollywood. Flipper's, however, was definitely the first celebrity all-star roller-skating country club. The hand-painted murals rimming the rink were topics of chit-chat around the Polo Lounge the way that wailing walls were conversation getters in Jerusalem. These phantasmagoric murals were as large as billboards. On the far wall, a portrait of Carmen Miranda rose in full glory, spreading into thousands of exploding bananas. On the middle wall, the big tropical one, artists had toiled to bring to life a vision of Henri Rousseau's tropical splendor — strange-looking lions and nymphs of King Kong glory roamed inside a surreal jungle. Some of the well-heeled regulars thought this was too California cosmic. Others reveled in the theatricality and referred to Flipper's as a modern merry-go-round. A setting in which fashionable crowds mingled, had a drink or two, sometimes snorted some of the evil stuff in the private lounges, and watched the spectacle of hundreds of skaters decked out in bicolored playclothes moving hypnotically to the upbeat music on the supra-sound system.

Just put your feet to the beat. Just put your feet to the beat. Picture this. You are lounging, lost in the magic of the floating panorama before you, on one of the charcoal banks of Flipper's. Social lion Swifty Lazar, the literary agent who is often spotted in the society pages, and his elegant wife, Mary, are engaged in frenetic conversation at the next table. Beside the Lazars sit a socially prominent black couple moving ecstatically to the pounding music. Her black, fine hair is twirled into masses of ringlets, and she is wearing a copy of a Sonja Henie skating costume. He is wearing an earring, a neon-blue cowboy hat, and Ralph Lauren cowpoke boots converted to roller skates. Across the room stand 500 hot and sexily attired people crowded together against the rails, the tropical bars, prepared to roller-skate with Mr. Right.

That is nothing, however, compared to the sight in front of you. Hundreds of skaters, ignited by the grace of their own choreography and flooded with neon beams, are twirling around the rink. There is something about this scene that is reminiscent of a Currier and Ives Christmas card created on acid.

A youth with Prince Valiant brown hair, wearing designer blue denim and workshirt prol chic, is rocking and rolling on his skates — throwing his feet into the pink lights. There is a blonde, lovely in a grapenut-flakes leotard, attracting widespread attention moving around the rink like a roller derby star. She is joined by a *Gentlemen's Quarterly* cover boy, a short-haired blond who might have stepped from a daytime soap opera like "The Young and the Restless." He is tearing the floor apart by engaging in somersaults. A hairdresser-to-the-stars in haute New Wave gear and wearing Lolita sunglasses, meanwhile, is doing splits on the runway.

Suppose you gave a party and *everyone* came. The cutie who posed for the Salem billboards. The lovely enshrined in American pop history as the reigning Virginia Slims girl. Los Angeles TV chat hosts Regis Philbin and Cyndy Garvey, the honey-blonde wife of Dodger baseball all-star Steve Garvey. Erik Estrada. Cheryl Ladd and Jaclyn Smith from "Charlie's Angels." Desi Arnaz, Jr. Rod Steiger. Ryan and Tatum O'Neal.

Flipper's was not merely a roller boogie palace but a piece of social theater. Some thought it was like rocketing to the moon.

Flipper recognized the Great Performances when he saw them. Flipper? Yes, there is actually such a personage. Since it *is* Hollywood, he has only one name. Like Fabian and Dion. Flipper's real name wasn't public knowledge; he preferred being a man of mystery and enjoyed being compared to fifties stars like Dion. Flipper, who was English, had come to California, he said, because Hollywood had been a magnet. He was fortyish and projected a paunchy masculinity. In London, Flipper had been influenced by a "B" movie called *Drive-In,* one of those beach-blanket epics released in the summertime for schlock movie devotees. He'd been taken with the roller-skating sequences. Especially the sections depicting Southern California roller-skating waitresses. Immediately, Flipper packed up his family — consisting of his wife, Caroline, London's Debutante of the Year in 1962, who had the Rolling Stones perform at her coming-out party, and their five children — and flew them to California.

Why not? Flipper's goal had been to entertain the international set at their various watering holes. In the Swinging Sixties it had been London. Although Flipper had been trained to be a gentleman at the finest English boarding schools and had dated royalty, he had become a regular at London's Crazy Elephant Club, dancing the twist with Joan Collins, fashion designer Mary Quant, and Hayley Mills. Flipper, in fact, had added his own special touch to English zany history. He had redecorated an old ship, sailed it off shore, and begun the first pirate rock-and-roll radio station.

Then the money moved to Spain. At twenty, Flipper had

become the chief honcho of a bar called Pedro's, in Malaga. Guests read bizarre publications and attempted to resurrect the glories of Hemingway's *Sun Also Rises* crew. Fondue and exotic cocktails, bullfighting, that scene.

Flipper's, however, was a crowning achievement in a career dedicated to erecting off-the-wall wonders for the modern age. California, Flipper said, was experiencing a Renaissance and Los Angeles was its capital. Sixty years ago there had been citrus groves and dirt roads. Now, the city teemed with eccentric pioneers of chic. El Lay had New Money. New Morality. Trends were starting there.

Boredom had always been Flipper's nightmare. Fighting boredom seemed to be the new national pastime in Hollywood. Flipper would wake in the middle of the night, wet, huge drops of sweat pouring from his round, nicely featured face, just contemplating living in a world filled with straight, middle-of-the-road types. But in Los Angeles, Flipper and the rest of the Europeans and New Yorkers who were flocking to California needn't worry about resistance to their dreams. Here was open season for invention.

Actually, Flipper could not roller-skate. Flipper had been maimed in an automobile accident and his right ankle would not support the four-wheel gospel. However, he had been trained to throw a theatrical event. Along with two other Englishmen turned Californians — Denny Cordell and Nicholas Cowan — he had captured the imagination of the media with a musical comedy roller-skating salon frequented by the cream of body-worshipping Southern Californians.

Amazing. When Flipper threw open the doors of what he referred to as his "little skating rink" in 1979, the upper echelons and their ever-faithful camp followers forgot Hugh Hefner's parties and Don the Beachcomber's brunch. In their secret heart of hearts matrons discovered they wanted to become roller-skating princesses. It got to the point where if you didn't skate you lost your social cachet. Society stars in Beverly Hills, Flipper heard, were paying youngish roller-skating champions $200 an hour for lessons on their tennis courts behind their mansions. Leaders of what was regarded as the "fun" group were building costly roller paths through the vast gardens of their estates. Giant corporation presidents were calling Flipper to book his skating palace for an evening. The pages of fashionable *Women's Wear Daily* frequently reported the coming and goings of roller-skating society.

Flipper had expected difficulty in capturing the attention of the attractive, young, trendy crowd which through their grapevine set the style in Hollywood. After all, there was plenty of competition from the natural wonders of the city. How do you top blue skies filled with spectacular clouds? Or sunsets at the beach?

But when Diana Ross walked into Flipper's one night, dressed in spangles and possessed of an energy which some thought Divine, the other overachievers quickly followed it.

Flipper's was not just a social phenomenon, but a cattle call on wheels. The new Schwab's drugstore discovery spot. Hollywood producers cast starring roles from the skaters on the rink. Television cameras recorded a new glitterati for the weekly TV newsmagazines. Only the prettiest or the most social or the most moneyed were allowed past the Amazonian bouncers at the doors.

Song. Wine. Stars. Sport. Beautiful women. Gorgeous men. Sugar Daddies. Flipper realized this was the unbeatable combination. Each night he arrived at the club and watched the brown, shiny limousines parked outside, their passengers bundled up in Attitude. Full lips tucked in so tight that every cheekbone looked like a Revlon advertisement. Their heads tossed in a certain manner, like the stars of Old Hollywood. They had attitude up the ass.

Flipper listened to their idle chatter. How Flipper's could definitely be improved if there were big mama hostesses dressed in Jamaican plantation gowns with barrels of fruit on their heads. How they'd hoped to see something unusual — like cages of animals. Monkeys on the ceilings, said one tycoon who had flown in on his own private jet, would be nice.

Still *they* came. Robin Williams had his birthday party at Flipper's. Teen idol Leif Garrett sat ringside most nights. Drag queens roller-skated toward the Art Deco powder rooms. James Coburn. Florinda Balkan, the Brazilian beauty/movie star. Christopher "Superman" Reeve. Bruce Jenner.

Paris Match was there, its representative recording another California phenomenon. *Life. People.* They all came to report what the designers-in-residence called the best "ass show" in the Western Hemisphere.

From the Copacabana bar, Flipper watched the extravaganza he had co-produced in the giant mirrors at the far end of the roller rink. Barbra Streisand and Barry Gibb were singing on the wall-to-wall sound system. It was a couples-only dance. There was romance in it. The most beautiful brigades of the year holding hands and plunging back to a more innocent time and at the same time toys in a pond.

The onlookers had vanished. Only the rollers remained. The rink filled with masses of Fiorucci-clad wonders. They lived for style. Flipper's attention focused on the girl in the yellow terry-cloth shorts and T-shirt and honey hair — an El Lay Girl of the Year — who had it all together. She skated with confidence. She was in a world of her own — not needing any other force but her own style to propel her into skating stardom. A skater nearby didn't have style. He was too stiff and rigid on the floor.

Then there was Cher. It was impossible not to notice Cher on roller skates. Her black, curly hair arranged in the manner of erotic figures on Greek vases. Her costume a panne velvet zebra-striped stunner. Her $600 skates hand-painted to match her outfit. Cher wasn't just skating, but floating on the stage at Flipper's like a prima ballerina. She had finesse. Unconquerable cool. She melted into the floor. With a combination of a star's presence and a *Harper's Bazaar* cover girl's pizzazz Cher led the pack as if she were producing an Emmy-winning TV special. Cher conquered Flipper's the way Cleopatra took Rome.

In the Bistro, a private dining area above the roller rink, Flipper would catch the conversation of Hollywood as the diners nibbled at their nonpreservative cherries jubilee. Sooner or later, as the night wore on and the diners loosened up, the main topics turned to dope and sex. Screwing with beer, two stellar stars were saying, was currently de rigueur. Carrying cocaine in Gucci bags, offered a starlet who had just became a sensation, her portrait gracing the cover of the *Star* that week, had become contagious. Between toasts to nearly every pretty girl in the room, two gentlemen discussed the latest sexual rites in the bedrooms of the stars. It seems the super-novas were placing cocaine on a thin, Tiffany stick, inserting it into their partner's phallus, and tasting the coke at the climax. Well, it was hardly fit for a status restaurant like Mr. Chow's. But it certainly cleared the tables.

Flipper locked the tinted doors to his roller boogie palace after the big Halloween bash. Inside, the hall was still vibrating with choruses of supersonic sexuality. The lights bathed the lonely rink in swimming pools of sensuality. The last cocktail waitress had skated to her cash register to tally up the figures for the night. The crews of roller-skating workers floated to and fro, picking up the refuse from the floors. Not everybody was into making the world work for everyone and against nuclear power. There were those who simply wanted to put the flash back into Hollywood. Give the Emerald City one last rush.

The cars streamed down Santa Monica Boulevard as Flipper walked outside and felt the chill of the California night. Flipper gave his obligatory greeting to the limousine drivers outside. He glanced up at the sky studded with stars. And he smiled. For Flipper had become a Barnum and Bailey's of the roller-skating age. If there was anything that Flipper had learned it was that no matter what catastrophe was happening around him — whatever holocaust in the headlines — people were essentially escape artists. It could be the worst of times.

But the majority still wanted to have a good time.

Flipper started his car. As he waited for the red light a group of roller-skaters flashed by. One of the girls, a blonde, stared inside the Mercedes. *Was it him? Could it be?*

Their eyes met. They smiled. Flipper watched as the light turned green, and he drove into the night. There were thousands of ways to make it to the top in Hollywood. This year it was roller-skating.

10 MALIBU - THE MOVIE STAR

THE MOVIE STAR GLANCED UP from her copy of *Architectural Digest* as her private Gulfstream II jet prepared to descend into Los Angeles International Airport through the rich bounty of white, fluffy clouds. It had been a turbulent flight from London, where she had just completed a film with Robert Redford. Suddenly the California coastline with its sandy beaches reminded her that she would have two weeks of rest before starting her next movie with Sylvester Stallone.

She traced from memory the coasts of Malibu below, the cloistered community where movie stars lived, and reviewed her own compound ($2 million when she bought it; $6 million now), complete with private pond and Greek statuary. The stewardess brought her yet another diet drink on yet another silver tray. She smiled the familiar smile that moviegoers had come to expect in their fantasies and awaited the stewardess's awed response. She noticed to the side her secretary napping against the Halston-designed upholstery of the finest Ultrasuede. In her Vuitton bag were the Valium 10s which would get her through The Session with

The Photographers awaiting her at the airport. She shook her full blonde mane and fastened her safety belt. It would be a long morning.

Five years, she reminded herself. That was all it had taken her to rise from an obscure starlet on a television sitcom to superstar. She felt secure, knowing that whatever happened now to her career — a flop, a bad director, an accident — she had made it to the top of the ladder. She owned a mansion in Beverly Hills. She had her own retreat in Malibu, the ultimate symbol of success. The world adored her. And thank God, no scandal had ruined her image as the prima donna of films. She wondered why she was not psychotic. Yet she wasn't. Her life was perfect. She held a mimeographed list of the day's events in her hand. Her sworn-to-secrecy servants awaited her every desire. Her husband didn't mind her being public property. She took care of herself. And even though few recognized it, she was very elegant. Very gracious. Very attuned to taking the training that accompanied success in Hollywood.

She needed exercise. She needed the serenity of the beach and horseback rides in the mountains behind her fifty-acre ranch. The private phone rang; the secretary put Richard Zanuck, producer of *Jaws*, on hold. She took the call and practiced the ancient art of public relations like a master of the form. Yes, Europe had been beautiful. Bob Redford had been a doll. Please send the script immediately to her house in Malibu. They still loved her.

The plane landed smoothly, falling like a bird of prey on the flattop of the private landing strip. A mirror was brought to her so that she could check out the famous face, which would be watched for any sign of imperfection. For some reason the Movie Star thought of Nancy Reagan as she prepared to make herself up as the image that Americans wanted to look at over their breakfast coffee. She had met Mrs. Reagan and Ronnie at the White House. Each of them, two women on America's Most Admired list, compared notes on legend making.

When she descended the ramp, the photographers sprang to action, screaming her name like football fans witnessing a spectacular 100-yard touchdown. It never failed to astound her — this rush that accompanied stardom. So many people considered it phony. She knew that. They figured Hollywood glamour had really gone out of style. But simply a slight switch of her marital status would become national news. A false step might make the wire services, a sign of stress cause women at supermarkets to grab for copies of tabloids. The Big Why came up for her. But she saw the answer in the faces of the photographers sprawled out on the runway before her. Femininity was only part of the answer. She knew dentists were lusting for her and placed posters of her Scavullo-photographed face on their walls. That the gay boys in their bars around the world worshiped her. But the secret lay in the face of a female photographer. She realized what stardom meant. It was the career choice of the decade. With hard work and talent you could manage to give yourself a life that few would ever experience. She made a difference in the world. Not politically, but in the psyches of the fantasy life of the nation.

Movie stars had seemed to go out of style, glamour become just another word in fashion magazines. But singlehandedly she had brought it all back. She predicted that twenty years or forty years from now she could still fill a rented hall with the millions who had found in her their ideal love object.

If only they knew, she thought, that it was even better than they imagined. None of the journalists who came to interview her — the Rex Reed bitchy breed or the moviestar mavens — could begin to imagine the total fantasy of what it was like.

The Movie Star stepped inside her luxurious limousine. The windows were tinted. The driver, her personal favorite, who had once worked for Princess Margaret, wore a gray, custom-made, London-tailored uniform complete with cap. He was smart enough to realize she didn't care to be bothered with chitchat after a long two-month shooting schedule. In the limousine she was inside her own private cocoon. She poured herself a sparkling glass of Perrier from the oakwood bar and relaxed.

The driver *never* drove the freeways. Instead, the limousine, a silver carriage worthy of a modern-day Cinderella, would tour the fantasy kingdoms of Los Angeles. Through the darkened windows, the Movie Star appraised the French fashions in the windows of the rich Beverly Hills boutiques, then settled back to view the palatial palaces of Bel Air as they passed before her hazel green eyes. At Sunset Boulevard the limousine glided along an avenue designed to dazzle spectators with its grandiose homes. She had been summoned by royal command to most of them. Now that period was behind her. *They* came to her.

Sunset Boulevard was one of her favorite California murals. On a clear day like today, it contained the gloss of a Great American Homes coffee-table classic mixed with splashes of nature, the envy of connoisseurs of Utopia everywhere. America was supposedly a democratic nation. But the game here was to see how unequal one could become. Living well was still the best revenge. The inhabitants of the residences along Sunset were rich, fashionable, visible, and sometimes well bred. The fun occurred in attempting to outdazzle each other with wealthy follies.

In Pacific Palisades, a golden community about ten miles west of Beverly Hills, she noted the car culture competition. Which Rolls was whitest? Which Mercedes had the most outrageous license plates?

All of this, of course, simply constituted a warm-up for Malibu. Sunset Boulevard wound down through the mountains and the modern villas to stop at the ocean's edge. Malibu was California's most private beach resort. And its richest. Along Pacific Coast Highway, from what was considered Malibu proper to Trancas, stood twenty miles of psychic reward for success. A Versailles on the Pacific. Malibu reflected an epoch in California history. A period in which the taste makers of Hollywood migrated from the city to the country, from the nitty-gritty to the mellow. Where the smart people purchased their own piece of nature.

There was Acapulco, of course. And Palm Beach. Even Newport. But Malibu set a style. Miles of cottages stretched like coloring book illustrations at the edge of the sea. Eccentric castles like facsimiles of Errol Flynn swashbuckler sets rising from the rugged mountains. Private driveways behind NO TRESPASSING signs, which ended at homes attended by four full-time gardeners, two maids, a houseboy, and at least one chauffeur. Lunch was served beneath umbrellas on an outdoor terrace, cocktails at palatial Mediterranean mansions, and formal dinners at beach houses with modern dining rooms.

The driver tapped twice at the crystal window divider, interrupting her reverie, when he stopped at the entrance to her beachside mansion to open the Art Deco gates, a gift from the Prime Minister of an Arabian oil-rich nation. She submerged into the luxury of the limousine and cuddled herself in her hand-knit Yves Saint Laurent dress. She loved the color. Mauve. She had selected a pair of $240 spike-heeled Italian shoes to match the dress. There was no applause as the limousine glided up the forest-laden driveway to her baronial retreat. The Movie Star didn't need any. Not today. Her portrait graced the covers of *Newsweek, Time, People, Life,* and the *New York Times Magazine.* She was back in Malibu. That was special. The climate guaranteed that every day would be perfect and that Kodachrome was promised like a postcard. The mountains behind her seemed to be her own private possession. The cult of nature was very fashionable.

Just the name, Malibu, was special. It meant movie star. Redford lived here. Barbra Streisand and Jon Peters. Cher. Sly Stallone and his golden girlfriends. Mary Tyler Moore. Natalie and Bob Wagner. Charlton Heston. Lee Grant. Goldie Hawn. Bob Dylan. Paul Newman and Joanne Woodward. Jacqueline Bisset. Diana Ross. Bruce Dern. Ryan and Tatum O'Neal. Dyan Cannon. Cary Grant.

A few years ago there had been a spectacular mudslide that catapulted Malibu onto front pages everywhere. Far into the sea were tiny dots of white which represented the sailing vessels of couples of the year. Yachts that featured her favorites — tricolored sails of red, green, and brown — the Gucci fleet. The homes were magnificent. Most of them natural, wooden mansions topped by weathervanes fashioned after the fantasies of the fantastic residents. Some were tacky. One featured a golden Oscar weathervane, which was considered a bit much by the more genteel residents.

The sound effects were terrific. Birds singing. Rustling winds. And perpetual quiet. You went to Beverly Hills to show off and be social. But you came home to Malibu for privacy. It was a retreat without Gray Line Tour buses, no fans allowed inside the oceanside compounds, no hangers-on admitted inside the monumental mountain spas.

Two bodyguards, incredible hulks who had once worked for the California Highway Patrol, watched over her as she gazed at the panorama before her and breathed in the rich oxygen of stardom. Malibu was the world's wealthiest outdoor insane asylum, she thought. Part of the thrill was the exclusivity. The press was verboten. Scandals not easily revealed. There was a locked-tight privacy to the Malibu elite. A glimpse at wealth so legendary social historians would speak of Malibu hundreds of years from now.

The Movie Star focused her painter's eye on her own estate. From the private helicopter pad to the pond to the main house and the two guest houses it possessed a grandeur which, according to many, was vanishing. The houses were starkly modern. She preferred the way it resembled her favorite Mexican Riviera retreats. The white stucco against the sea and mountainsides giving it the cast of a tropical plantation in a surrealistic Mexican painting. There were no weathervanes. Only stark, cubic lines. At dawn it looked primitive. At dusk like a castle for the space age. She had given orders. It was *never* to be photographed. Never to be displayed in architectural books. Garbo wasn't the only one who wanted to be alone.

Inside, the servants gathered to greet her. The main house occupied two levels — and each room was cavernous. Fresh flowers were placed everywhere. As well as paintings from her own private collection of Picassos, Matisses, and David Hockneys. (Hockney, an English artist, had painted breathtaking portraits of Californians against turquoise swimming pools splashing in water colors.) The furnishings were muslin tropical. She had attempted to create a personal hotel superior to any hotel in the world. Friends said the Movie Star had succeeded.

No matter who you were, tea was poured at dusk. Breakfast, served on silver trays, consisted of poached eggs cooked exactly the way you requested, whole-grain wheat toast with butter, and your monogram on the hand-loomed linen.

She expected the Jacuzzi, off her bedroom through the tinted-glass doors, to be ready. So she immediately passed through the spacious living room, through the library, which contained the first proofs of her autobiography, and climbed the stairs to the bedroom. She let the maid undress her, and descended into the bubbling waters of the primeval pool. Jets of water caressed her body.

There was nothing to worry about. The maids were answering the phones. Secretaries separating the hangers-on from the *muy importante* who's who hoping for the pleasure of her company. The Movie Star usually went full tilt. Up at dawn, breakfast, business meetings, studio work, luncheons with journalists, late-afternoon shopping sprees hopping from boutique to boutique in Beverly Hills, and late-night conferences with producers and her business manager. Today she could afford to relax.

Although her life sounded exhausting, it wasn't. Everything was always handled for her. Every detail of the day programmed. At one time, she had been anxious about everything. Money. Gas. Bills. Stardom. Cars. Insurance. Romance. Sex. Today it was all taken care of. To acquire something new, all she need do is ask for it. She didn't even worry about the journalists. They loved her personality. Some even suspected that beneath the preconditioned responses to the preconditioned questions there was a hidden reserve of privacy which she shared only with a chosen few.

A star. It was not only being gorgeous, dressing gorgeously, and acting gorgeously. It meant charisma. The ability to execute entrances and exits of such exquisite grace that your presence burned into memories. The Movie Star was not a vague reminder of the age. Rather, she was the personification of the dreams and values of her generation. When she stepped into her perfumed sunken bath, women everywhere got a hit off her private fantasy. When she shopped at a store, it suddenly became special. Did she cook? She didn't have time. Did she want children? In time. What was her opinion of women's lib? Call Jane Fonda. Because of a quality under the painted exterior that suggested to people their own sense of hidden glamour, she had been allowed to become a Great Lady. Currently she was so powerful she didn't even need the talk shows. Or the personal appearances. She didn't have to worry about *anything*.

There were unexpected views of the Pacific Ocean throughout her home, her favorite an I-can-see-out-you-can't-see-in sauna. She found herself always smelling of cedar when she steamed there. The maid toweled her down. As she stepped into her bedroom, she glimpsed in the mirror her all-year tan and admired her full breasts and firm bottom.

The bedroom was not highly decorated, as was the fashion this year in Malibu. But it contained an exotic eighteenth-century Chinese wedding bed, one of twenty in the world, plus a fireplace and mirrored closets full of the childhood fantasy gowns befitting a love goddess. The tinted windows of the room were constructed to make the blues of the sky outside appear bluer, the greens and golds of the garden outside more lustrous, and the sparkle of the sea below more dazzling.

Many worshipers of the Malibu dream supposed that the residents lived only in bathing suits. In truth, many of them were full-timers on best-dressed lists. A package had arrived from Charles Gallay's exclusive boutique in Beverly Hills, a shop in which the Italian and French frocks carried price tags marked down to $900. As one of the world's foremost conspicuous consumers, she had her own private style sessions, with the owner in attendance at all times. The proprietor was graciously cautioned to inquire first before releasing information on any of her purchases to the press.

Friends, beautiful friends, were arriving for lunch. There would be talk about Princess Caroline, who was resting at the beachside residence of a friend in the Malibu colony, the closest thing in California to Hyannis Port. But most of the table talk would center around the Movie Star. Her latest projects. Her newest acquisitions. Strictly off-the-record. And if one told, one wasn't invited back.

She wore a brooch designed exclusively for her by Salvador Dali, and she welcomed the admiring eyes of her guests as she joined them for lunch on the terrace. The lobster mousse was perfect. And the wines fine. The guests included three other movie stars, and she was acutely aware of their competitive gazes. There was a polite commotion over the lavender, pink, and blue Porthault linen. Many compliments for the cooks, a Chinese couple she had borrowed from Cary Grant for the summer.

If you intended to become a star, you'd better know how to play the game. It was an exclusive sisterhood in which each one of the players attempted to outglitter the others. To stay on top one had to outdress, outmarry, outspend all the others. She wasn't concerned about her friends, who currently accepted her as the grande dame of the group. It was the others, inspired by her legend, who were willing to take the whole movie-star trip to higher heights. It would be a long climb.

The Movie Star was at a point now, in the company of a few other giants, where she wasn't obliged to engage public relations patrols to exploit her sizable achievements. A movie star, by her definition, was any performer who could account for a box-office profit regardless of the quality of the enterprise in which he or she appeared. The breed was growing scarce. Clint Eastwood. Streisand. Paul Newman. Redford. Burt Reynolds. Brando. She was only in her early thirties.

She took a sip of her espresso and reveled in the scene before her. She adored the emerald green mountains. The Decorous Life of Malibu. It was the only important American resort where dinner jackets and evening dresses were rarely seen and almost everybody who was anybody was asleep in his or her king-sized bed by midnight. The residents flaunted informality. The homes were really fairy-tale wonders, homage to the pages of the *Whole Earth Catalog* built on million-dollar scales. Jeep Chic was fashionable this summer. And dogs. Not just your common variety Palm Springs poodles. But Great Danes and German shepherds. It would soon be time to spend long, lazy afternoons with her closest friends in the white-tiled barbecue room filled with blooming orchids. Or meet with her husband on the beige suede sofa in the library, where the false-front bookshelves opened by remote control to reveal a bar and a bathroom decorated in brown and gray velvet.

There was absolutely nothing to do. Nowhere to go. And that was the way the Movie Star wanted it. Strictly low profile. What was referred to as the Malibu village was simply a hastily strung out collection of neon-lit hamburger stands, a couple of magnificent cliff-hanging seafood restaurants, an old pier, and a mission-tiled shopping center where the servants picked up the bare necessities. Everything of any value was imported from the outside. There wasn't even a cemetery. But, after all, nobody came to Malibu to die. They came to withdraw from the pressures of legendary fame. Malibu life often felt like the inside of an expensive sanitorium, but she liked it that way. She was grateful that her days were no longer filled with the clutter of luncheons, dinners, cocktail parties, and benefits. That was for the climbers like the Beverly Hills matron who was gaining recognition in the columns because she had hired her chef from Maxim's. The Movie Star *chose* to live behind closed doors.

After her guests had departed, she was free for the day. Rare moments alone. She cherished the solitude after two months in the limelight. Even with the tightest security, she had still been surrounded by constant crowds everywhere in Europe. Everything *had* gone beautifully. She was still front row center in the world's imagination.

She informed the servants she didn't care to be disturbed. She would take the opportunity to enjoy the magnificence of her own home. The new bamboo furniture, which reminded her of Polynesian thrones, was wonderful. She planned to browse through magazines, phone friends, cook something. She needed some reality after all the unreality. In Paris she had watched fans line up in front of her portrait on billboards high atop theater marquees. In London she accepted an invitation from Buckingham Palace to be presented before Queen Elizabeth. Now, she must have two weeks in Malibu just to recharge her batteries.

She fingered the Valentino upholstered walls in her bedroom as she changed from her luncheon frock to a $400 hand-tied Christian Dior silk robe. She felt marvelous.

Descending the stairs she realized this was her best role. She threw open the doors of the library and picked up a copy of *Casa Vogue*, an elegant home-furnishings magazine from Europe, and gave herself the luxury of another world. The best homes, the most attractive people, the most fantastic decor entertained her eyes. It was all available to her. Did she want to meet the Duchess of Windsor? Why not? Dr. Gucci requests your presence at a very private showing of fall furs in Rome? All right, Aldo. She had instant cachet with the world's most stellar personalities. After all, she was The Movie Star. After an hour of selecting treasures from the magazine, she switched to *Elle*. The California fashion industry had changed in the past few years. No longer did you have to fly to France or Milan for couturier clothes. Everything in the French magazines was available at the designers' boutiques on Rodeo Drive. It was a taste revolution, and she had been at the forefront.

By the time she finished with the fashions, almost certain that she would not be wearing a short skirt next fall, she was hungry. She walked through the two high-ceilinged drawing rooms to her kitchen. She could see the Pacific Ocean through the sliding-glass windows. Sea therapy — she had read about it somewhere. Well, anyway, it was true. Every time she walked along her private beach or sat in her gazebo by the sea at sunset watching the vermillion skies years would drop from her life.

She found some broiled chicken in the refrigerator, tossed a green salad. She had forgotten the lushness of the menus in Malibu. The refrigerator was stocked with favorites like partridge with foie gras and truffle stuffing, eggs and caviar, chicken stuffed with gold leaves, and filet of sole stuffed with caviar. The wines ranged from a pink Dom Perignon to a Chateau Lafite from the Rothschild vineyard. Dinner in hand she moved to the terrace outside. The late-afternoon shadows cast spells over the placid oceanfront. She hardly needed paintings. Malibu had some of the most dramatic landscapes in the world. If you could pay the price. The private beaches were available only to the highest bidders.

Her husband was out of town on a business deal, so this was going to be a quiet night. She called her closest girlfriend, who listened attentively to the European stories. Trust didn't come easily in Hollywood or Malibu. Once you got past the first thrill of stardom you reached a point of never being certain who was recording your conversations for a scandalous exposé. She felt better after the phone call. Her energy restored, she decided on a swim before bed. The bodyguards stood atop the cliffs as she entered the warm waters and with smooth strokes found herself far out into the private bay. She felt the tension vanish. She loved the way salt water made her hair thick and welcomed the divinely blonde highlights from the strong sun. She was lost in her own private piece of the Pacific, feeling as if she was either the first woman in the world or the last. She didn't care. She felt Alive. Energetic. Resplendent.

When she returned to the compound for exercises conducted at the house by a Beverly Hills exercise specialist, she was on a high. She had always loved the adventure of her own body.

She climbed into her Chinese wedding bed and watched through the gigantic picture windows of her boudoir the moon pass between cherubic clouds. This was ironic, she thought, a star gazing at stars. The Movie Star watched as the heavens lit up before her eyes. It was a weekday; everyone in Malibu would be in bed by ten. Tomorrow, the limousines would glide like wagon trains toward the studios. The sisterhood would be studying their scripts in the back seats, sipping whatever got them through the day. At night, the star trek would return to deposit the gods and goddesses of the American empire at their personal fantasy kingdoms. The hot-tub tycoons and their nonpreservative mamas of Malibu.

She picked up her Pentel pen and a sheet of paper from the top of a tortoise bureau. The Movie Star made an addition to the galleys of her autobiography. She wrote two sentences: "They thought that romance was dead. But it really wasn't." In the distance she caught sight of a huge yacht lit up for a party at sea. Listened to the pounding waves outside. Her agents were handling her deals. A studio flack her publicity. A business manager her career. Fifty years from now she imagined someone reading a copy of her book. They probably wouldn't believe her. Yet it would all be true.

11 NEWPORT BEACH—THE MATRON

6:00 A.M., NEWPORT BEACH

How to give a blow job. Deborah was playing at *fun* titles for her new novel about Newport Beach. She — a sunbaked survivor of the battle of the sexes in the fun-in-the-sun paradise — was sitting on the sand at sunrise, watching the late John Wayne's old multimillion dollar yacht sailing forth into the crimson clouds. Her blonde bouffant coiffure had been done regally for her beach meditations by the *best* hairdresser in Newport. This blond beachboy did hair from his garage in Laguna and provided hatha yoga training during his blow-dry session. He also came up with some wonderful lines for *the* novel. "Fuck Rodeo Drive — if you want status, baby, stick to Newport Beach hairdressers," he had screamed this morning over his pounding disco tapes. Deborah had rushed to her Cadillac Seville to jot it down in her notebook. She had to write a best seller, she thought, as she draped her well-maintained thirty-six-year-old super-vixen frame on the warm sand. Her first version of the title had been *How to Give a Blow Job.* Stark black and white cover, Deborah fantasized. But that wouldn't do. It just wasn't respectable.

And the survivors of the rich retreat by the Pacific would cast stones at her fine form. But, my God, there was a story here. Ari and Jackie had never sailed forth for Newport Beach. But a lot of tycoons who could buy and sell them had. Deborah knew where *all* the skeletons were hidden. She could almost hear the resounding, exploding overture right now. Of course, they would make it into a movie. It already was a wonderful trashy movie, the kind that Deborah would rush to see — her favorite being *The Other Side of Midnight*. (When Marie France-Pisier put that coat hanger up her twat, Deborah had let out a howl of delight.)

She stood now on the beach, the wind playing dirty tricks with her frozen hair, and pictured herself as a beach-bunny Scarlett O'Hara. In front of her, laid out like a waterpainting, was Newport. The rich, green hills covered with homes with adobe roofs shining in the morning sun like gold. The science fiction towers of Fashion Island, *the* shopping center for the status-starved natives, jutted up out of the landscape like a space tower. To her right she spotted Promontory Point, a vast conglomeration of singles complexes resembling an Indian reservation, and saw the revelers hitting the Jacuzzis. To her left was the majestic residence of the Balboa Bay Club, where corporation presidents traded in their gray flannel suits for jogging gear and surfing trunks and stood at the windows of their beach villas as they dialed their cronies on the East Coast. "My God, you should see it here," they would scream in their best Boy Scout voices. "There's a blizzard in New York, right? But it's sunny and blue skies here."

The weather, the beach, the topography made Newport Beach paradise. The Easterners had what Deborah called the *fix*. The feeling. No matter who you were, Newport would get inside you like a treasured snapshot.

This was the American way, she thought. All the games

and visions of the society transformed into an outdoor spa. She counted the resort's attractions. The "Father Knows Best" homes built next to perpetually green golf courses. The sleek sailing toys decorated with shining chandeliers and wall-to-wall bars. The recently built sailing clubs, watering holes for scandals and broken dreams.

It *was* a novel. Because ten years ago, when Deborah and her husband — a darling man into hydraulics — had arrived in their white Cadillac convertible with red upholstery from the San Fernando Valley ("Smogsville," Deborah dubbed it), Newport had been mainly lima bean fields. Now it was a boom town. With a style all its own. Deborah changed into her uniform — *very* Newport Beach — blazer, tight corduroy trousers, and Charles Jourdan shoes — placed two or three Ferragamo gold chains around her neck — and started the motor of the Seville. She felt right. She had kept up. In the mirror she saw the charming Wasp princess of the fairytale retreat. Charm, Deborah thought to herself, is a lost art. So is graciousness. People were big on graciousness in Newport Beach. The parties. She hated them. But she had to attend them, because that's part of her job. They provided contacts. She had to keep up a front. That meant don't wear a plunging neckline like that dumb fool Marian. If you have to flirt, do it the way people did in those Cary Grant pictures in the forties. Doesn't that tell you everything about Newport Beach? Don't mention marijuana and don't whisper cocaine. Deborah drove off into her sleek, lush day. She was bored. It was time to see her psychic.

---

10 A.M., BIG CANYON

Deborah relished coming home because she knew that nowhere else — not St. Tropez or Rio or the Caribbean — was there anything to compare to Big Canyon. Just the name made her feel like Barbara Stanwyck, the eternal western mother earth figure, a gun-totin' mama saddled up and rarin' to go. She cherished the Big Canyon parking shield on her Seville. When she would glide through the lush shopping centers, or shop the little boutiques with their colorful terracotta facades, she observed the flatland women noticing her shield. Big Canyon meant something. It characterized the Dream. Deborah had no anxieties about making it. She had made it the minute she and her husband bought the faintly French mansion, which Deborah chose because it was an exact replica of Billie Jean King's home. She didn't have Billie's gazebo, but Deborah complimented herself daily on the fact that living in imitation of a superstar in the community caused her star to rise higher in the horizon. Five years ago there had been no Big Canyon. But land developers, noticing the incredible marketing figures on Newport — that more corporation presidents and vice presidents lived in the lush ghetto than anywhere in the U.S. — decided that they would go for broke. They would create out of nothing the ultimate California planned community. The whole town would be organized around a golf course with a huge brown, modern, wood clubhouse. The homes would be modeled on every traditional American style ever featured in *Architectural Digest*. The homes would start at $2 million, and that investment alone would turn a profit for the lucky few who would be hand-picked, chosen to homestead in the luxury community of the future. Those land developers had been tremendously savvy, to Deborah's way of thinking. Because they had predicted that Newport was ready to become a world showplace of enormous wealth and status. They had created what Deborah called an instant wow. From the immaculately groomed entrances, which featured small chateau-like guardhouses, to the rolling, winding roads that passed through the residential wonderland, it all resembled storybook land. Bubbling brooks would come out of nowhere gushing with water, birds singing nearby. Little creeks flowed past your bedroom. Always you could see the colorful golfers and their striped-roofed golf carts in the distance — an advertisement for the good life.

Deborah could certainly appreciate the amusing side of this blissed-out wealth. Sometimes she thought she was living in a reincarnation of *The Loved One*. Sometimes, she mentioned to a well-read girlfriend, she wondered why the developers hadn't called the community Forest Lawn South and erected an imitation Last Supper at the eighteenth hole. She didn't treasure ending her days on a golf course. And she detested the fact that the clubhouse — one of the most spectacular summits of California's pursuit of leisure madness — featured a men's grill from which women were barred at the power breakfasts or lunches.

The quality that Deborah loved about Big Canyon and all the other retreats rising from the barren earth in Newport Beach was that they presented another form of the California way of life. Her European and Eastern friends expected Newport to be another one of those way-out affairs where everyone talked of "getting clear" and "mellowing out" and rushed to women's consciousness groups and read *Zen and the Art of Motorcycle Maintenance*.

Deborah had done some bizarre things — in and out of her beloved Missoni sheets. She had gone to faith healer Kathryn Kulman years back, and this miniskirted messiah with the most incredible bob of hair since Carmen Miranda placed her bone-thin hands atop her princess crown. But that was about as "born again" as the Newport mobs could stomach.

Women were allowed psychics. Deborah and a couple of her more adventurous friends would bring a group of these underfed, rather grotesque spiritual advisers up to the Good Earth Restaurant and feed them expensive health-food cuisine and await their lofty pronouncements of future shock. The nobility that Deborah rubbed shoulders with didn't worry about such things as exploring their options and getting their act together. They *had* their act together. Their performances were encrusted in cement. The men were heterosexual, thank God. If women allowed them to have their adult toys and to roam freely through the bedroom communities once in a while, there was a marriage. Life was a perpetual George Segal–Glenda Jackson movie. There was alcohol. There was divorce. And there was maintenance.

Deborah was on a natural high as she parked next to the Big Canyon clubhouse, which she gave a quick once-over. Tremendous design. This building possessed the exquisite lines of a Japanese tea garden blown up for a barbecue. She liked feeling her Charles Jourdan pumps hit the gravel, which was cleaned daily and was like a red carpet to the desirable people who would be getting soused inside. She threw open the wide, oak doors (Deborah referred to them secretly as the King Kong doors) to step onto a set of the ultra-suburban dream. The huge windows looking out on the golf course were tinted so that the view had an unearthly gloss to it. She avoided the golfers because they reminded her of death. Reminded her that some day she would hit what was laughingly referred to as "the better half" and shuffle off to glory with a hunky Marine type carting her Vuitton golf bag. She studied the play clothes of the guests sitting around exquisite banquettes drinking expensive Mexican beer. *So* California. She liked the fact that out of heavily Chap-Sticked mouths came the gruntings of raw sexuality.

They were in an alcoholic haze, these people. There was even something rugged about the way the men offered powerful prose straight from *Hustler*. And the women couldn't care less. They had it made. There were weekends up in Palm Springs dining with Betty and Jerry Ford and planning political comebacks. There were the endless Supermom wailings about the dental atrocities of their Master Race children. The graceful sweep of the roof, the plushness of the carpets, the immaculate silence of the staff. Deborah ordered a Bloody Mary, flirted innocently with one of the waiters, and reached for her own private phone. But Kitty was not at home. *"No en casa,"* the Mexican maid had offered. Deborah let out a howl. She realized that this was probably the most profound remark about life today in Newport Beach.

===

NOON, JOHN WAYNE TENNIS CLUB

This was Deborah's idea of tennis. She was lolling in the sun rubbing Borghese sun gel — the *only* kind to use, the others are just imitations, Borghese is the pure stuff — over her fabulous fifties form and watching the daily flotilla of regulars run through their paces at the John Wayne Tennis Club.

Ten years ago, Newport had been filled with a squadron of retired World War II admirals and generals. The big topics of discussion had been World War III and what were Richard Nixon's chances for reelection. Today, Newport was a lush, tropical version of "Peyton Place." The women were climbing toward social and sexual status in the community. The corporate presidents were building empires and enjoying adultery in the sun. Everyone discussed the families who controlled the resort — the Irvines being the number-one celebrated name that could cause ripples of anticipation in listeners at the staunchly Republican clubs and dinners. They would have to figure in Deborah's book somehow. Because Newport was one of the few areas of the country outside Texas where old cattle baron–like Western families could still sit on their ranch and control thousands of bulldozers and contractors in their pursuit of turning Southern California into the master-planned tract home of the future. God, did the men talk real estate down here.

The other historic change was the rise of the movie-star population. When Deborah had first encountered Newport the only topics worth mentioning were the weather, the hunky men, and a couple of eccentrics. She had been fond of the bizarre reports of one socialite who took her orphanage duties so seriously that she was constantly leaving home and fortune to cruise around the poorer sections of Orange County looking for urchins to swoop into her gray Eldorado, kidnaping them for fabulous picnics and sailing soirées which, according to the grapevine, cost her over $4000 a week. Such Mrs. Miniver types vanished, thank God, once the movie stars and the corporation presidents moved into Newport. Now, it was a scene.

Raquel Welch was a recent resident. Newport had Arabian sheiks in residence. Abdul this or that, snickered Deborah, touching up her coiffure and catching the reflection of her golden legs in a glass door at the club. There was one sheik, in fact, who was said to have ploughed every woman on a certain block and was now busily accumulating conquests in the deluxe bedrooms of Big Canyon, Deborah's own Shangri-la golf community where the dollhouse homes — all very American looking, nothing exotic — were going for nothing less than $2 million.

Money was flowing. Deborah would wager that many of the executives heading *Fortune*'s top 500 had visited Newport in the space of the last six months. It was safe. No man wore a haircut that would cause concern in the executive suites. Most of the wives were good sports — the type who read the sports page each day even though they couldn't tell the Super Bowl from Tidy Bowl. Deborah detested both sports heroes and politics. She was so tired of hearing that perhaps Jerry Brown wasn't so bad after all that she would retire to the powder rooms, the ones with the pink quilted doors, and listen for gossip of a more sordid nature. But then, you had to keep up.

Her book, she fantasized, could be a kind of sun-drenched *Atlas Shrugged*. There were a lot of strange corporate philosophies being reported at the dinner parties. Most of the men and women in Newport were waiting for the all-American industrialist to sweep them up in his Sedan de Ville and transport America back to its Golden Age. Deborah also hoped to bring back patriotism. The Fourth of July was a religious holiday here. Flag waving and red, white, and blue golfing regalia were daily sights. Most of all, however, Deborah loved the trash. What entertained Deborah was chronicling the rise and fall of the scandalous corporate kings. Lesser souls — more timid and reserved — would have become blabbering Lois Lanes interviewing these Supermen of American power. But Deborah thrived on the drama that was developing here because the glamour of the location and the glamour of the money had produced a generation of movers and shakers. One false step and everybody in the whole goddamned Newport Beach would lose their parking shields for the tennis and sailing clubs and be banished to trailer court retirement in Dante's Inferno or lower Laguna Beach. Deborah knew all the false steps.

"Do you think anyone will be here?" asked the tennis club hostess (a little too full figured for Deborah's taste) in her brightly striped uniform as she dropped off some Perrier water.

"Honey, *everyone* will be here," Deborah answered, wishing that Barbara Walters might appear to record her comments.

Deborah tried to imagine how TV cameras would view the scene. She fantasized the opening shot: Walters standing in front of the huge $1.5-million sports spa surrounded by the Mercedeses, Jaguars, Super-Vans, and Jeeps; the cameras zoomed in on the famous John Wayne western brand featured on almost every wall, doormat, and tennis shirt offered at the club. It was *so* "Duke"-ish. And *so* Newport Beach. All the people here were really like human cattle. They lined up at the spas or the stores to purchase the brands that would give them status in the community, would make them instant princess and prince of the Southern California leisure world.

Deborah then surmised that Barbara would say a few choice words in that mannered voice of hers about the fact that the club had been built by Wayne's ex, Pilar, and that memberships were sold for as little as $3000 and reportedly as much as $15,000. She also surmised that Walters would be bright enough to entrance her viewers with the knowledge that the club resembled something out of a sci-fi epic. Inside were the 1984 touches of electronic scoreboards, computer scorecards, and the eight statuesque hostesses. (Deborah was sure *that* would elicit some of the famous Walters bitchery.) At the same time, the club was a throwback to some kind of luxury ranch where men of the West could take comfort in the brown and green decorated clubhouse, the masculine relics of Wayne's cowboy movie career, and interminable patriotic platitudes by Wayne. "If every American would just get down on his knees every morning and rise and go out to do something for their country then we would return to the days of Plymouth Rock." It was the Knott's Berry Farm trick, thought Deborah. Newport's architectural gift to the world of design. Make it super-modern, make it so preposterously electronic and space age that the citizenry could practically see UFOs each night and at the same time sock it to them with the Declaration of Independence decor. Seventeen seventy-six meets Buck Rogers.

Next, Deborah imagined the TV cameramen would focus on the huge, eight-foot bronze statue of a young tennis player in the central court — Newport's version of Rome's *Three Coins in the Fountain*. Natives literally worshiped at this shrine. There were a lot of conservative, wealthy communities in America. But few spread out their materialistic beach towel with the toys available in Newport. Including crotches. Women bedded tennis instructors because in their lean, tanned, muscular bodies they held the plasma of youthful romance. The IBM businessmen filtering around the statue found in the tennis player a hero. Forty years ago it was Babe Ruth; today it was Jimmy Connors.

Deborah recognized that beneath the Brooks Brothers facades the men were adventurers. They moved here to create a Walt Disney adulthood in which life was a perpetual dream. They were game players. And that made them darling and very beddable.

Deborah was sure that a few seconds of camera time would pick up the dazzling display of the rich court life. The middle-aged executives and their wives battling it out, the birds singing in the hills as their background music. Such a world had been the late John Wayne's. He had come down here like the rest of them for the paradise treatment. The incredible massage of the soul of living with the Super-Nice society, the desirable communities and the saga of the sea. In the pages of sailing magazines, and the tennis quarterlies, Newport had become California's Riviera.

God, country, and sports — that was all you needed. And a couple of legends on the order of the Duke. The place was so historically romantic that Deborah was surprised so many visitors missed out on the vision being produced in Newport. It was the new Adidas royalty and John Wayne had been the Duke, his club had been his Buckingham Palace. Everyone missed the Duke so much in fact that after his death they changed the name of the airport to John Wayne International.

Deborah noted several of the older wives drinking on the sidelines. Alcoholic wife stories were worth gold on the party circuit. It was the one thing that could cause a divorce quicker than wife-beating. Wife-beating? Well, some of the women loved it. It was their thing. The soaps all day with those gorgeous TV princes, then getting beat to a frazzle at night because they didn't care for Monday night football.

Deborah was bored. Walters and the TV cameras didn't arrive. The dumb attendant had brought her only a story about a stockbroker who traveled to Hollywood each week to have a $200 call girl give him what is called in polite circles a Golden Shower. The stories Deborah knew. Someday she would give a charming sit-down dinner party for eight or so and call it a Genital Torture Night. Right now she needed a drink, and she refused to be seen imbibing in public. Carefully, she folded up her reading, her gel, and her ultra-sunglasses, placed them in her Vuitton bag, and headed off into the sunset like Joan Crawford playing Mildred Pierce. Maybe there was some material at the homestead. God, she hoped so.

---

5 P.M., BIG COUNTRY

Nothing. Deborah checked menus for a dinner party later that week with the maitre d', who looked like a "Gunsmoke" crony and didn't know the first thing about French cuisine. Deborah decided to go for a drive up at her secret place in the hills above Big Canyon.

The first time she had cruised up to this spot it had taken her breath away. Here she could maintain her dreams of manifest destiny by looking behind her at the virgin fields alive with golden-orange poppies and realizing that more of this kind of life was about to sprout up in this wilderness. Here she enjoyed peace of mind from getting close to the land. Here she gazed on Balboa Island through binoculars over her immaculately done eyes and focused on the kiddieland called Newport below her, bathed in gold from the sun.

She zoomed in on a Newport stud bicycling along in the fields, his knapsack on his back, his powerful legs bronzed almost to the glow of his hair. Two years ago he would have worn sweatpants and gray sweatshirt. Now he was aglow with racing-stripe colors. She caught the *Ziegfeld Follies* show at the high school track, the young men and women racing along like athletic chorus lines. She focused on the sailboats and the yachts aloft in the giant Jacuzzi of the ocean. She turned up the disco music on her FM stereo. Something about "Do ya wanna be a hot number?" She picked some gloriously golden sunflowers for her living room. All the striving was behind her now. She really must get to work on the novel. She cast the main character as a Kirk Douglas type, an executive, who reeked with power and controlled incredible amounts of land and political power. A man's man who had the frame of the Herculean possibilities of Newport. His wife, an Ava Gardner type, was at his side, building their corporate marriage to a pinnacle of style and taste as well as knowing every sexual trick in the book and then some. A girl, a "Charlie's Angels" dental assistant, maybe, would climb into the relationship, destroying it because she cherished everything the wife had — including her husband. There would be several minor characters. The screaming queen of an exercise king. The ski instructor who teaches the wife about dominance. There would be volumes on plastic surgery and a lot about creative divorce. Deborah would relish it all. After all, Newport Beach was the perfect soap opera. The perfect women's novel. From this immaculate cleanliness and facade of superniceness Deborah would find the trash that would make a best seller. "Do you wanna be a little hot number?" the radio asked again. Oh, yes, thought Deborah. And then some.

12 BOYS TOWN – THE WEEKEND

SUNDAY

There was an orgy, of course. Every Sunday afternoon poolside party in Boys Town had its bacchanal. Blackie Norton's, however, far surpassed the others. Not only was it More Beautiful. More High. More Exclusive. But more political, more star-studded, and much more difficult to crash than the others of the lesser Boys Town moguls. You had to be on a Super-A guest list and clear yourself with Blackie's secretary just to get past the sentry dogs and the barbed-wire security fence surrounding Blackie's $3-million fairy-tale castle in a hillside section of Boys Town notoriously known as the Swish Alps.

There was sex. Blackie never denied that he provided Hollywood's most glittering array of stars with the best of the boy beauties who came to Boys Town. But you could get sex anywhere. Your name was not placed on Blackie's preferred list just for fun and frolic. You had to work the joint.

It was one of the greatest casting couches in Hollywood. Blackie's poolside nocturnals were at the very center of El Lay's homosexual world. An invitation to Blackie's was considered so important that appointments for sex-change operations were hastily transferred to other days. Blackie was devoted to status, people, and party giving. Not to mention blackmail. The more horrible a guest's reputation, the better.

Inside Blackie's doors lay another country, designed to beguile and dazzle and tempt. Layer upon layer of fantastic rooms collided. There was a salon for the leather boys, a salon for western and cowboy aficionados, a chandeliered ballroom for rich queens who believed that they were Lana Turner and Rita Hayworth reincarnated, a room of exotic bamboo ceilings and surfboards for the beach-boy contingent. The crowning achievement of Blackie's extravagant homosexual fun house was an entire salon layered with shields and coats of arms out of the pages of King Richard and the Crusaders. A one-time beer baron, who should have been too smart to become involved with the likes of Blackie Norton, supplied the liquor. A steel heiress, who had a passion for other women, supplied the elegant suppers of filet mignon and caviar. It cost once you entered Blackie's never-never land.

Blackie's taste for opulence fit wonderfully into the American homosexual dream. The whole Sunday afternoon gangbang was summed up by a brilliant painting which dominated the grand entrance of Blackie's main foyer. It pictured naked men, ravishing little things, climbing atop each other on a palm tree. Blackie Norton's Camelot on the Pacific might have been flavored tutti-fruity, but they didn't call him Daddy Dearest for nothing. The boys of Boys Town knew what a Sunday at Blackie's could mean. Discovery. The chance to finally become a star. The guests intended to climb the gay stairway to heaven for all it was worth.

Blackie would *have* to look great. His hairdresser, the

same man who claimed he cut Liza Minnelli's locks, had come early that morning to style his hair in a loose perm — a look that was very popular among the young of Boys Town that summer. Blackie spent an hour under the sun lamps perfecting an even tan. He was beaten to a pulp by a masseur who had once demonstrated his techniques for royalty. But Blackie's foremost pleasure in life were two-hour facials from a charming Frenchwoman who was said to have kept Brigitte Bardot young. Blackie was only thirty-two. But anyone past twenty-four in Boys Town was labeled a senior citizen.

The old studio system was dead in Hollywood. But gays like Blackie Norton liked nothing better than to be pampered like the old movie queens. Immortality, Blackie always said, that's what made Boys Town tick. Each occasion was a movie sound stage, and on the film of memory you could live forever.

Blackie Norton waved the barrage of servants from his presence. He stared at himself in the mirrors of his purposely overdecorated bedroom. He told himself he was the richest and handsomest man in Boys Town. Over and over again. Waiting until his blue eyes gleamed with sensuality in the wall-to-wall mirrors of the room. He was ready. No one said that narcissism didn't do wonders for your complexion.

———

Liberty was cruising Robertson that morning. Robertson Boulevard in West Hollywood from Beverly Boulevard to Melrose Avenue had been dubbed Fairy Lane by Boys Town gays. The split-level bungalows owned by the interior decorators and the lovely home furnishings shops gave the area the appearance of an artist's colony. But Robertson was a notorious gay pick-up spot. You could find almost any form of erotic entertainment within its confines. From dungeon rentals to bikini dancers. From genital torture to Golden Enemas. There were hard drugs and aphrodisiacs. There were pushers and prostitutes. Robertson Boulevard was a very long way from Kansas.

Liberty was aroused by the scent of vice and crime. He knew that Robertson had a dangerous reputation. He had read the series of articles in the newspapers about a doper in a green Chevy van who picked up homosexuals on Robertson street corners, tied them up in the back of his van, and watched them O.D. on heroin while he filmed their death scenes for foreign distribution.

Liberty was also privy to inside information that it was an addiction to Robertson and not Hollywood's star system that had really injured a popular young TV actor. The star had simply found a sexual gimmick that was too much for his sensitive system. Sometimes $35 bought you more than a cheap sexual thrill.

Liberty had been a landmark on Robertson for two years. He would leave practice late in the evening and drive crosstown in his yellow construction worker's truck. When he hit Melrose and Robertson he would turn left, and from then on reality didn't exist.

Liberty knew the rules. Robertson was a drive-in sexual supermarket. Traffic jams formed most nights from eleven to dawn. On Sundays all day. Homosexuals would roll down the windows of their automobiles and sexually proposition other homosexuals cruising around in their cars. They needed to be picked up in the worst way.

Liberty spotted a number on the street; he was leaning against a telephone pole. The stud was staring at Liberty lasciviously. The stud had a Marine Corps short, cropped haircut. He wore an earring in his right earlobe. Bulging arms. He looked like he drank beer in a leather bar for a profession. He did not smile when Liberty cruised him. He sneered. The famous gay bar sneer. It was modeled after tough guys like John Wayne storming Guadalcanal. Paul Newman in *Hud*. Don't fuck around with me, it said. Of course, it meant exactly the opposite.

There was nothing in Boys Town's rule books that said homosexual love couldn't be beautiful. Or that two men shouldn't fall in love completely. Hollywood screen stories had often presented the gay soap opera as tragic. But that was only in the movies.

Class ass, Liberty said to himself as he crossed through the party to greet his host, Blackie Norton. Liberty was aware that he looked splendid that night. He was pleased that he looked his most professional. Blackie Norton threw a high-class gay act. The banquet on the finely designed tables was sumptuous beyond most upper-class cuisine standards. Mimes passed out the silver plates for the exotic foods. The waiters had been borrowed for the occasion from the most exclusive restaurants in Los Angeles.

Blackie Norton treated his guests like noblemen. Many of them were much more than that, Liberty noticed. Some of the richest gays in the United States had been invited to the party. From famous heart surgeons to orchestra conductors they flocked to Boys Town and Blackie Norton's to be introduced to their latest boy-wonder lovers.

Liberty wandered outside to the Roman pool area with its hot tubs and Jacuzzis. A crowd of young men had gathered in bleachers around the pool area. On key, rising from the pool like Esther Williams in her MGM heyday, a black entertainer, Tweety Pie, entertained. At exactly that moment, however, Paradise and Michael showed up. Liberty was interested.

Very interested.

A hung hang-glider in full flying regalia was now entertaining around the pool. They called him Wings. But who knew what anybody's real name had been in the world beyond Boys Town? Blackie Norton did. Blackie kept extensive files on all the guests at the party. Not only typed Manila folders. But filmed video cassettes. Right now behind the mirrors of the rooms full camera crews were recording the events at Blackie's for posterity. At a future date Blackie would sell the best footage for fortunes to his own gay network of rich executives around the world. The one thing that visitors to Hollywood dreamed of was making it with a movie star. Blackie could not always arrange that. But he could sell them films of their favorites at play.

Paradise was now in full camera view. The zoom lenses of the cameras caught his perfect profile. However, Paradise was lost. Every man at the party desired him. No. Paradise did not want to go to dinner with a couple of high-priced TV comedians who had come to the party dressed as the Lone Ranger and Tonto. He was totally uninterested in playing kneesies with the grandson of one of the founding founders of Hollywood. He was not amused by two hairdressers who called themselves General Electric and the Rear Admiral.

It wasn't Paradise's fault that he was so beautiful. It was always the same story. Everybody else — all the other boy beauties — lost points when Paradise arrived at the party. Suddenly insecurities flowed like tap water. The competition was looking into mirrors and finding themselves not okay. No one in Boys Town ever bothered to look into his own interior mirror. This was Hollywood. The Beauty Capital of the World. When you had it like Paradise all the doors opened. If you didn't, you paid to see it on the movie screen.

Which reminded Paradise. He had come to the party to use his beauty for better and better work. He now had the perfect opportunity.

The private zoom lenses now cut to Silver. Silver had been in Boys Town only two weeks. He was a successful Canadian theatrical producer. Silver had big bucks written all over his fashionably trim frame. He could offer Paradise one of the leads in the biggest all-star Hollywood epic since *Grand Hotel*. Silver was gorgeous. Very debonair. An original — highly original — swinger. He also put out something that none of the other men at the orgy had offered Paradise. Romance.

Blackie Norton couldn't have been more pleased. He watched Paradise and Silver retreat into a private bedroom for their business negotiations. The elite in Hollywood claimed that deals weren't made in bed. Most people in Hollywood were liars.

Blackie would make a dividend from their contractual settlement. The filming of their private lovemaking would clean up at the home box office. Blackie knew the one way to gauge a big financial clean-up. When Blackie Norton couldn't wait to see it, then it sold. Blackie also had no idea what the breaking point was in Paradise's sexual chemistry. But he was excited about the prospect of discovering the secret formula.

Michael was now free for Blackie's high-voltage assault. Blackie enjoyed nothing more than initiating newcomers into the kinkier styles of gay love. Michael was alone.

Blackie could offer most of the world to the boy. Gay men worshiped success. There was more buying and selling of flesh in Boys Town than on the New York Stock Exchange. Men like Blackie could afford the most desirable male fantasy. Freshness like Michael's was one of the big marketing pluses. Blackie and Michael mounted the stairs to the master bedroom.

13 THE DOPE DEALER

NOON, BEVERLY HILLS

This was about the funniest trip in Ricco's life. But he couldn't laugh. This was not a laughing matter to the poor bastard standing in the bathroom stall with him. This gentleman, whom he'd seen in one of those fashion magazines — this big industrial mogul who always had his picture in the Los Angeles business columns — was actually shaking. He did not know who the score was because Ricco's contact — this doped-out salesman over at a menswear store on Rodeo Drive — had arranged the meeting. But here he was feeling like Julie Christie going under the table to give a blow job to Warren Beatty in *Shampoo*. The place: this incredible Beverly Hills restaurant full of status people. Walking past the French maitre d' and up the stairs to the men's room, he had spotted Gloria Swanson, the ultimate old movie queen, and some minor league celebrities. Ricco had shown up at the men's room with his Mark Cross briefcase and had been sitting in the stall waiting for a tap for ten minutes. Some old guy wearing fruit boots had gone whacko. He tried to beat the door in and was outraged. But he wasn't the score. The score would be wearing Gucci shoes. When he tapped on the stall door Ricco let him in and told him to shut the door quick. If anyone came in Ricco would jump up on the toilet seat and instruct the score to pretend to "take a piss." It was obvious that the society figure had never scored cocaine before. And that the man — a Gregory Peck look-alike — was scared. But Ricco thought the whole trip was wonderful. Comic. Here he was standing on a toilet seat opening up his suitcase full of baggies full of grams of cocaine, and before him in a beautiful $500 Dorso worsted suit was one of the most powerful men in Beverly Hills. Anyway, the score didn't know from dope. That was one thing Ricco, one of the biggest dope dealers in Beverly Hills, was sure of. When he told the executive, "That'll be a C for a C," the man had looked at him in bewilderment. The dude was buying cocaine only because he had met some hot chick, a Jaclyn Smith look-alike, who wouldn't make it with him until he scored a gram of coke. "I mean, that'll be one hundred dollars. Cash," Ricco explained. The man had pulled out an alligator wallet, handed him a C note, thanked him, and left.

Now Ricco was heading for the Daisy on Rodeo Drive. There he would pass himself off as a real estate agent. First he had a couple of errands. He wanted to check with the parking lot attendants and the limousine drivers along Rodeo to see if anybody had come around that afternoon desiring to score. No one had. Ricco stopped to admire himself in the mirrors of Vidal Sassoon's hair salon. Yes. He had the John Travolta look down pat. He was older than Travolta, perhaps thirty, but he didn't wear a tie and his thick chest hair stood up against his navy blue Bijan suit.

Ricco kept thinking about his score as he slipped into a

seat, sunning himself at the outdoor café at the Daisy, and watched the regulars pass by on Rodeo. There was Britt Ekland. A few other Hollywood stars. Ricco ordered a Robert Redford health-food sandwich — turkey and avocado on whole wheat — from the waitress, who looked a little wasted today, and asked her, "You wanna snort, honey?"

"Naw, you got any speed?" she answered. "That woman over there with the burgundy hair is a real bitch. She probably hasn't been laid for over two years and she's taking it out on me." The music inside the Daisy, a hot spot in Beverly Hills during the evening hours, when it turned into a private club, was pounding. Ricco felt good.

God! What in the hell was this? Walking down Rodeo, the status street for the past few years in which he could watch a better fashion show than the ones he'd seen in Paris or London, was this eccentric dressed up as a status Christmas tree. He smiled and waved a candy cane at the Daisy regulars, who were applauding his performance. Weird dude, thought Ricco, but just like everybody else in this town. Looking for some thrills. The eccentric handed Ricco a card informing him that he gave private performances of his Christmas tree act night or day at premier functions. Suddenly, Ricco felt like a joint. This was going to be an insane day! He slipped into the Daisy's men's room and from a gold Dunhill cigarette case he took a J.

Upper-class people, thought Ricco, as he returned to his seat in the sun and looked out at the spectacle of Rodeo Drive in full Thursday glory. How had he ever gotten here? It was a long way from Whittier, California ("Huh," laughed Ricco, "Richard Nixon's hometown"), where he had been born in February 1950. Along the way, he'd changed his name from Mike to Ricco. Mike had no class. It was all right when Mike scored in high school. It had been all right when he had gone to Vietnam. But five years ago, walking down Melrose Avenue, wearing his jeans and white T-shirt, he'd been picked up. It had been Mike's ultimate fantasy. To make it with a movie star. He wouldn't reveal which one — that would be tacky, and one thing he had learned in Beverly Hills was you just couldn't be tacky in public. His movie star, however, had taken him to one of those mansions the tourists view when they buy maps, to guide them to the stars' homes, along Sunset Boulevard. Suddenly he was in her bedroom snorting coke and sniffing over-the-counter butyl nitrate from a bottle labeled "Rush." She had sized him up, he remembered. Charm, good appearance ("Honey, you look like a movie star"), intelligence, but no money, no political power, little wit, and no class. "I don't usually make it with surfer boys," she said. "If you want to stay around here you're going to have to change your name and change your act." It was then that he had become Ricco.

She had dropped him in a week and gone off to Acapulco with a drag queen, one of Beverly Hills's flamboyant florists. This was decadent, he had thought at the time. But something in him enjoyed the outrageousness of it all. Through a guy he had met in the army he scored some cocaine on commission. With a suit purchased on credit at Saks Fifth Avenue (not the greatest label, but okay for a young, rising executive) Ricco had started his climb. Phony business cards from one of the better stationery stores listing a phony real estate firm. The Mark Cross briefcase with the sacks of cocaine inside. He began to hustle Rodeo. Beverly Hills was a weird town, he thought. Underneath all the glitz and glitter and the status labels, Ricco sensed the insecurity of the women and men on the street. During his jaunts in his chauffeur-driven limousine up into the hills to deliver his $3000 (cash only) cocaine supplies to the wealthy, he often ran into CPAs who admitted that their clients were worth a half a million, but didn't have a "pot to piss in" due to high living.

Ricco loved being high on Rodeo at the Daisy. He considered it the best way to appreciate the street. On dope he could relish the spectacle of stores that didn't resemble stores, but seemed like art galleries of fashion — especially Gucci, Ricco's favorite, which in its streamlined splendor and all-gold exteriors resembled maybe the most elegant movie theater in Paris. They treated you like class at Gucci, even the heavy-duty doormen.

Ricco never used dope as an escape, only as entertainment. On a high Ricco imagined himself as Charles Boyer or Marcello Mastroianni in the romantic movies which he watched in his private screening room in his gingerbread mini-mansion in Trousdale Estate.

Generally men didn't interest Ricco. Rodeo, however, had become a hot homosexual pick-up area. There were hordes of hairdressers in tight black trousers with status sweaters (Valentino Vs were hot, he noticed) wandering about trying to catch the eyes of the straighter male types strolling the streets with their girlfriends, mistresses, or wives. Also passing by were old men in white Cadillacs with gold jewelry dangling like Indian spirit shields around their chests. Big Daddies, thought Ricco. Everybody was on the make on Rodeo Drive — that's part of the spectacle. Including the shopkeepers who waited outside their doors in resplendent suits of the finest European wools and silks waiting for the latest busload of Japanese tourists.

The European men were role models for Ricco. They had a kind of savoir-faire, and Ricco jotted down notes on what they said, how they ordered, their expressions as they viewed the female spectacle each day on the street.

Above all, women were Ricco's passion. He had a prototype in his mind. Someone like Mrs. Robert Stack, whom he had seen driving down Rodeo in her Rolls-Royce Corniche. She was a Golden Girl with soft, silky, long, luxurious blonde hair, flowing European clothes. The way she moved along Rodeo — as if she owned the whole street and still got a kick out of it — appealed to Ricco's newly acquired sense of the absurd. He wondered what her insecurity was. That was the only way to approach these kinds of women — to find the fatal flaw in the beautiful exterior.

Leaving a healthy tip and a joint under the check for the waitress, Ricco hailed his limousine and sped off into the afternoon sun. He took off his Bijan jacket, laying it on the richly upholstered seat. He stuffed a Bee Gees recording, "Spirits Having Flown," into the cassette player. Removing a baggie of cocaine from his briefcase, he used a razor blade to cut himself lines of coke on a mirror. Cocaine reminded him of baking powder — which his mother had used to make birthday cakes for him in that horrid home in Whittier. He wouldn't think of that now. He was rich, he had class, some wit, intelligence, but no political clout. He would work on that, thought Ricco, as the limousine climbed up into the hillsides above the Beverly Hills Hotel. Power was everything in this town. He didn't want to turn out to be just another servant. Another gentleman-in-waiting to the rich. Someday he would ring the doorbell of that movie star and astound her with the fact that he was somebody. In this town it just didn't figure to be a nobody.

The limousine glided into Sandra's driveway. "What do you mean bringing *him* here?" Sandra, a red-haired woman in her late thirties with decals on long fingernails, was waiting in the living room of the old Spanish house she shared with husband Harry and two children. She was mad. She yelled, "Are you *insane?* Bringing a reporter here. My God, you're going to have to have us all in jail, you crazy fool!"

Ricco was total charm. "It's cool, baby, it's cool. Relax."

"Don't tell me to relax, you bastard."

"Let's go into the bedroom, baby. I've got a little surprise for you."

Like clockwork, Ricco manipulated Sandra onto the stairs and they climbed arm in arm into the upper areas of the old home.

The home was a prime example of celebrity real estate. Sandra would say later that she had done what she could with it. The goddamned place had been haunted for one thing. The children would dance wildly at night awaiting the ghost of the former occupant. She had added Beverly Hills touches. Oatmeal furniture. White carpets. And Ricco, whom Sandra had met one night at dinner at Morton's Restaurant when she was feeling particularly vulnerable. There was nothing wrong with her husband. Harry was successful, charming, attentive. But he was getting old. The disease of Beverly Hills. Sandra had become nothing but a svelte, babbling accessory to his tennis games. He had married her for her game, she found out later. Her husband, a banker, had needed a good player to establish himself as a regular on what was referred to in the columns as the "A" tennis set. Sandra, a former model who gave up when the agency asked if she could dance nude, figured she had it made. She would take Extra-Strength Tylenol in the morning, Valium in the afternoon, and Librium at night. It seemed to be working.

And play the game. The kids came. Then one day she woke up feeling that the fun had gone out of her life. She couldn't stomach Rodeo Drive, for one thing. It was totally plastic. She preferred off-Rodeo shops.

After all, shopping was the only game in town. Or facials at Aida Thibiant. Aida had these incredible machines which Sandra sank deep into during the afternoon. Then she exercised with the other women at Ron Fletcher's salon on Wilshire. The damn parking — about $8 for a day — got her down. But she didn't have a Corniche. The Beverly Hills meter maids gave you a ticket if you didn't have a Corniche.

Sandra had always felt insecure anyway. She wasn't a movie star. She wasn't one of the women who appeared each week in the pages of *Beverly Hills People*. And her past — God, what a past. She had been born in Fresno, one of the Bible-belting farm communities of California, too many years ago. When Sandra hit El Lay, a charmer claiming to be a photographer had picked her up at the beach. He loved her cheek bones! Nobody had ever loved her cheek bones before. So naturally she fell in love with him, and he photographed her and pushed her into the top West Coast modeling agency. She just didn't have the commercial look for photography. The top money accounts went to the blonde, surfer-type girls who specialized in bouncy California charm which sold all those endless McDonald's burgers and bottles of 7-Up. So she picked up work from some of the designers in downtown Los Angeles, names so obscure that when she mentioned them at chic parties other women smiled blankly. No Galanos, for God's sake. Or even Rudi Gernreich. But it was her ticket out of Hicksville.

Those first Beverly Hills parties had been horrors. Sandra learned that although everyone pursued exaggerated lifestyles — extravagant habits beyond her Fresno background — many of the men were very conservative. And very boring. They talked almost exclusively about business, and thanks to the charm courses she could hide the yawns. The younger men took her to dull bastions of Old Guard money palaces like the California Club.

Sandra forgot Fresno. She had even caught the eye one night of Otis Chandler, the tycoon of the *Los Angeles Times* dynasty. But it was only eye contact. By the time she met Harry, he seemed like the best choice. At least he was athletic. Yet she woke up one night and felt this... depression. She knew that something was missing.

Every once in a while there would be a glimmer of hope. Some big event in Beverly Hills society where she could glitter brightly, attracting a few photographers. But Harry didn't earn the kind of money to move with big society spenders like the Alfred Bloomingdales, of department store fame. Motherhood was wonderful, but all those fairy-tale stories lacked a happy ending.

When she met Ricco at Morton's, the room seemed to part as in a romantic song, and there was only this beautiful figure of a young man, a man right out of the fashion magazine ads she hid in her bathroom and which she could masturbate to with the shower hose. He followed her to the parking lot, he followed her in his limousine to a McDonald's restaurant. She got inside the limousine. He produced a joint — the first she had smoked in her life — and she was into an entirely different world. She was giggling uncontrollably. An old man, a beggar, knocked on the window and asked for spare change. When they rolled down the window, laughing wildly, the old beggar smelled the aroma of marijuana and vanished. Sandra fell in love.

Ricco and his dope had started as a game. She was totally in control of the affair, she said to herself. Sex should be for free and for fun, just like her psychiatrist counseled. But that bastard, the shrink, didn't know the first thing about dope. Or about youth. Or about the beauty of a young man. Young skin. Hair so thick that at night she could feel her hands running through it, combing it in fantasies of every new form.

Ricco and Sandra returned to the living room. Sandra was wildly stoned. Suddenly she filled the house with music. Not Mantovani. But hard rock. "Crank it up," she yelled. "Crank it up."

The light was harsh and the beginnings of age were evident. Sandra had maintained herself with tennis and with Fletcher's exercises, though she no longer had the bloom. But under the influence she felt young. She danced. Ricco managed a perfect John Travolta imitation on the dance floor. He knew what Sandra wanted.

Ricco could only take Sandra when she was high. He liked the fact that she was such a lightweight. That a few snorts of coke or a joint could produce this childlike innocence. But she had no power. She couldn't get him anywhere. Ricco just enjoyed being her young stud fantasy. And her $1000-a-month habit.

Soon, the chauffeur would honk and he would dance off. Sandra would let him. The radio announcer said: "Welcome to the land of love, joy, happiness, and kindness. And anything else is a violation."

Ricco had to make a score.

And Sandra had her tennis game.

14 THE TEEN IDOL

THE ULTIMATE FANTASY. The reporter was sitting down to lunch with an authentic California teenage idol. The star, only seventeen years old, was already the host of his own syndicated teenage talk show, a recording artist who had an album in *Billboard*'s top LP chart and a television series in the family hour top ten. It was reported that he had earned $1 million last year.

The Teen Idol, one of the richest kids in Hollywood, told the reporter that he would have loved to have taken him to McDonald's ("everyone hangs out there"), but instead they were inside the Teen Idol's favorite place in all the world — a pitstop Greek hamburger stand in the middle of a shopping center in the San Fernando Valley. The star was chomping on something called a guruburger. It cost $1.75, or $2.10 with french fries.

The Teen Idol was oblivious to the fact that few of the customers at the roadside stand, decorated like the Greek version of a dive in *The Godfather,* with lots of plastic hanging grapes, had noticed his entrance. But what did adults know about teen idols? What did adults know about *anything?* He wasn't big on glamour. He picked up a brown cafeteria tray and stood in line with the rest of the suburban patrons of the fast-food palace. The only break in his nonchalant, have-you-ever-been-mellow California facade appeared during an incident involving his publicist and the cook at the Greek restaurant, a sumo wrestler type.

"I'd like a Perrier," the publicist, a fortyish, fashionably dressed, balding man, requested.

"We only have Cokes, 7-Up, and Diet Pepsi."

Well, it was going to be that kind of day. But the reporter had a job to do, a lifestyle piece for a national magazine on the Teen Idol. So he asked the wholesome superstar if he remembered Vietnam. But the Teen Idol had been six years old when the protest was at its height. He looked up from his pita bread and hamburger concoction. "Uh-uh. No."

The Teen Idol had also, as it turned out, never dined at such four-star restaurants as Scandia and the Bistro. He considered such questions bordering on insanity. "Hey," he said brightly, "maybe we could all get back into my Chevy van and go cruising down Van Nuys Boulevard. Or go see Cheech and Chong at the drive-in. I've seen them three times and I know what they mean about not going to see them straight." (Wink. Wink.)

The star is like, antsy. He's been on the phone all morning with reporters from Miami, plugging a concert. He didn't have to go to school that morning.

"School is a bummer. I get the worst grades. I had straight fails in the seventh grade. All I did was screw up. I mean, my friends and I just ran up and down the halls during classes egging teachers in their faces and lighting firecrackers in the class."

So much for education. The Teen Idol threw an olive

into his California-cutie mouth and invited everyone to eat up. But he had news. "Hey, I'm going to record another album. That'll be hot. But it won't be punk. That's a real passé thing, that punk."

The best thing in his opinion that he could do — the real blast-o thing — would be to cruise around in the van and stop in front of young girls just out of school on bus benches; he'd go right up to them, smile, jump back into the van when they recognized him as their teenage hero, then run from them when they began screaming. "That's great," the Teen Idol said, oozing good-time charm from every cell.

The reporter wanted to know what it's like to be the Teen Idol?

"I don't know what the hell it is," the golden-haired instant sensation with the masterpiece orthodontia mumbled. "All I know is that I get up there on stage and thirteen thousand girls roar if I just put my face outside the curtain. All these girls are dropping like flies all during the concert. They can't breathe. Once I decided to be real cool and I jumped off the stage; I jumped right into the audience and they just went all over me. I got my vest torn off, and they all wanted to, like, touch my hair or something."

Didn't the Teen Idol love the articles in *Tiger Beat* and the other teenage fan magazines? "The only time I read that stuff is when I get curious to see what they said about me. Then I look at the stories and go, 'My God, what bullshit.' "

It must be nice to receive sweet letters from his fans.

"Sweet? They're weird. It's not 'I Love You,' and all that. No, it's right down to 'Let's go to bed, my phone number is . . .' You know."

Then the Teen Idol, piling french fries into his kewpie-doll mouth, told the reporter about his family life. "I had a normal life. We never did anything different. The only thing my family did is move into bigger and nicer houses. We've moved ten times in the last ten years. The last two years since all this teenage idol stuff have been nutso. But up to fourteen I've done anything and everything anybody else would have done. You know, my sister and I stayed in our house with our mom and went on vacation once a year. Things like that. My friends and I did terrific things. We egged houses at night and drove around on our motorcycles when we weren't supposed to. We'd build go-carts and make underground forts and jump off our house into mattresses. I guess we did everything."

The Teen Idol decided to blow the Greek burger joint. But not before a confrontation with the publicist, a man still in an advanced state of future shock from riding in the back of the kid star's van to the restaurant. "If you don't shape up I'll have my mom speak to you. From now on, I want a limousine at the airport to pick me up when I arrive in my private plane. And hire somebody to pay the bills for the lunches."

He ordered the publicist back to the house and instructed the reporter to jump inside the van. He turned on the radio, producing some rock-and-roll on an El Lay teenybopper station, and played an Alice Cooper song at a thundering decibel. The Teen Idol *loved* his customized, Darth Vader, black metallic painted van. "Hey, I got a Blaupunkt stereo amplifier with a JBL component speaker," said the voice of the new technology. "I got a three-foot speaker in the back." He called it the Blob.

The van, which had tinted windows so that no one could see inside, came fully equipped with taped cassettes of rockets blasting off from Cape Canaveral and flashing Christmas-tree lights which simulated sci-fi jet propulsion chambers.

"You know what I'd like?" Now the Teen Idol was

screaming over the outer-space racket, as his foot revved the accelerator of the van to full throttle. "Just to be looked up to as an actor. I got a part in a TV movie. I mean, a good part. But I'd like to be somebody like Paul Newman. You know, respected as an actor."

The Teen Idol drove past a succession of shopping malls, endless miniature golf kingdoms — a valley street lined with fast-food outlets and instant trees.

He directed his van toward Ventura Boulevard, which was out of the way, but he wanted to show the reporter the afternoon's movement on the main thoroughfare of the San Fernando Valley, an affluent, residential area protected by mountains from El Lay's metropolitan basin, and considered Teenybopper Heaven. A rock group on the radio chanted, "I'm on the highway to hell. I'm on the highway to hell." It was not yet four. School was out. The streets were packed with gangs of teenagers drifting from red light to red light on the palm-tree-lined avenue. The street had a kind of pink majesty. At night it was lost in a sea of fire-red, gas-blue, and electric-green neon. But by day the pastel colors of the restaurants, bars, flower stands, and the bizarre boomerang facades of the supermarkets and car dealerships designed like Spanish missions gleamed in the golden sun.

The Teen Idol had an urge to stroll down the air-conditioned corridors of a nearby $100-million space-age shopping mall. Even though it was December a heat wave made it scorching hot inside the van. His apparel, however, was totally climate-conditioned. Like most Southern California teenagers he always looked as if he was dressed for the beach. He had his shirt off and wore only tight-fitting, blue corduroy shorts and, of course, Nike tennis shoes without socks. On second thought, the shopping center wasn't such a bright idea after all.

They drove past streets filled with stereo shops shaped like

Fort Apache and finally came to rest at an ice-cream emporium designed in the manner of the Matterhorn. The Teen Idol bought the reporter an ice cream cone, soaked into chocolate and dipped into nuts by a salesgirl dressed like a turn-of-the-century dance-hall hostess.

"You shouldn't be depressed." Chocolate dripped from the Teen Idol's mouth. "Just cause you went through that Vietnam thing." (The reporter had explained about the Vietnam War and why many people were upset by it.)

So to cheer the reporter up, they jumped back into the van, and he drove into the hills to show off his latest acquisition — a white Colonial-style mansion where he planned to take up residence when he turned eighteen. "Around here there's a party every night."

"This is going to be *your* house?"

"Yeah, it's on an acre of land, and it's got corrals for my horses. It's got black wrought-iron gates that surround the place. It's got four bedrooms — all redone. It's got the bitchingest staircases in the most blast-o house I've ever seen in my entire life. That's a lot of house. You won't be able to see inside from the road, and that's the way I like it."

"Do you know how much it costs?"

"This house, one million bucks. I mean, that's how much it costs. But you only have to put one hundred thousand dollars down and you make payments every month. I'll be working a long time to pay that sucker off."

It was turning twilight, the clouds a jet stream of unearthly pink against the ink-blot blue sky. It was decided that they should continue the interview at the valley home the Teen Idol had purchased for his mother and sister a few months ago.

"I'm going to get hell at home." But as he drove the van into the night, off the freeway ramps and along the tree-lined avenues, he could cope with the traumas of the teenage star set. He seemed to find escape via the upbeat babble on the radio. "Hey, hug something or somebody today in the City of Angels," purred the laid-back voice of a disc jockey. "It's Hug Somebody Day in Los Angeles."

When they arrived at the expensive, sprawling ranch-style hillside home, nightfall was fast approaching. The view was magnificent, the lights of the flatlands below shining like a collection of neon necklaces. The Teen Idol was anxious. A fleet of Cadillac Sevilles, one of them owned by his mother, was parked in the driveway under the fragrant eucalyptus trees. In his rush, a football exploded under the rugged, huge wheels of the van.

"Sunuvabitch." It was too late. Almost immediately, his mother, looking like Anna Magnani on a bad night, burst forth from the house. She was not amused. The mother was about forty. Her fashionable Missoni dress and Maud Frizon shoes quivered with rage as she spoke. She was a small woman with a boyish haircut, which was all the rage among valley matrons that month, but it was obvious she didn't stand for any star bullshit *at her house.*

She had a powerful effect on the Teen Idol. Immediately he dropped the pseudo-masculine facade and became the bad little boy. He spent twenty minutes cleaning the cement driveway from the refuse of Frisbees, skateboards, auto parts, and bicycles.

Grabbing the reporter, he warned, "Play it cool." They entered the house. The Teen Idol had just completed signing a new million-dollar TV contract, but the house, although expensive, was decorated in a style that could only have been called California Awful. Avocado-green-shag-rug, wall-to-wall carpeting. Cottage-cheese ceilings with tinsel highlights. Fake Greek archways painted in thirty-one-flavor pastels. What had happened to "movie star" homes?

The Teen Idol apologized to his mother and nonchalantly

sprawled against a leather easy chair. From there he could overlook the Olympic-sized pool outside. Lit up at night it looked like lime Jello. The mother, meanwhile, sized up the reporter. After a few minutes she handed him her current philosophic handbook.

The mother, pleased that the reporter was "open," left the room to join her friends, who were bringing in packages from the cars and the day's shopping expedition to nearby Beverly Hills.

The reporter asked to see the Teen Idol's bedroom. The star opened the door and smiled. But instead of the den of iniquity promised in the pages of the teenage fan magazines, it was PTA approved. The Teen Idol slept and did all those things young boys did at night, not on an orgiastic waterbed but a plain and ordinary single with a citrus green chenille bedspread. The only sign of worldliness in the room was a stack of *Playboy* magazines in a corner. Other than that, the decor consisted of a clock radio, a couple of lavender-lit posters, a huge Teddy bear collection, and a group of miniature plastic horses. There wasn't even the prerequisite teenage stereo. *This* was Hollywood?

"I receive ten thousand letters a week. But I don't answer them. I have a company down in the city that does all that stuff."

The Teen Idol's soft, shiny blond hair fell loosely about his cherubic face. His eyebrows were well shaped and set off big, icy blue eyes. Someone had said that he was androgynously beautiful, but he didn't understand what that meant. Without the aid of a dictionary, he thought androgynous was a new rock act. He didn't go in for that culture shit.

At some point in their fantasy lives young girls would imagine the Teen Idol bundled up in ski clothes schussing down the slopes or riding horseback without a shirt while his bronzed chest took on the warm glow of the sun or motorcycling through canyons, his hair and shirt blowing in the wind. Such fantasies didn't faze him.

"Look at my *Playboy* magazines. Boy, I'd sure like to spend a few hours with Miss January."

The Teen Idol wasn't interested in literary enlightenment. "I don't know if I'd like to read your article. I never did do well in reading and stuff like that. It's a drag, outside of *Playboy*."

A Mexican maid, dressed in a bright shawl and a blue housedress, brought them munchies. The woman was clearly terrified of all gringos. She spoke no English. The Teen Idol only spoke teenybabble. The mother was full of psychobabble. The publicist spoke Hollywoodbabble. The only thing real in the house seemed to be the furniture.

"So what do you do with your nights?" the reporter inquired.

"There are a lot of party people around here." The Teen Idol perked up. "You just go cruising in your van down on Van Nuys Boulevard and ask 'where's the party?' I go to about three parties a night. None of that fancy Hollywood stuff. That's too yukky. All those searchlights and stuff. But *real* parties. The bitchin' kind that go on until you hear the police helicopters flying around outside. The valley is the party capital of the universe."

"What about, well, girls?"

"I have only one rule. I never go out with fans. They're just Oz people. Somewhere out in outer space. Most of them look at you all mushy-eyed and they're so scared of you that they're no fun. I don't go out with Hollywood girls like Tatum O'Neal or Brooke Shields either. They're so busy working they don't have time for *boys*. The girls that I like are the ones who have never heard of me. The *real* cold ones. The ones that pretend that I don't exist. They're a challenge."

The reporter was finishing his interview, but the Teen Idol wanted to show him one last treasure. Real man-to-man shit. They left the house, emerging into the warm California night. Some of the Teen Idol's neighbors were already inspecting the local landmark in their vans and yelling catcalls at the richest kid on the block.

The Teen Idol didn't pay any attention. Besides, he was too excited about the next blast-o moment. He opened the carport to show off his barbells, a collection of auto parts, and expensive tools. "This is where I really live." He enthusiastically picked up a wrench and walked over to the van, lifting the hood and giving way to all his repressed auto-shop fantasies.

One million dollars per annum. The Elvis of the post-Vietnam teenyboppers. The current bubble-gum king. Fans flocking to see each nostril quiver, each eyebrow arch. Loved. Adored. To hear his voice, to see his vast open-sky smile meant everything to twelve-year-old girls who traded in their Barbie dolls for his autographed picture.

The Teen Idol was still smiling as the reporter said good night. "Hey, don't feel bad," yelled the idol of the new generation, the cutest and the richest seventeen-year-old in California. "Maybe I'll even get an Oscar. Wouldn't that be neat?"

15 THE SHOPPER

11:00 A.M., BEVERLY HILLS

Nancy Czar is in bed with Jackie O. Not *the* Jackie O. Onassis. It's Nancy's dear Tibetan terrier, whom she has named after her all-time favorite woman. "The woman whom I met and was stunned to find out was just a real human being and so down to earth." Jackie O — gray, with a sad face and a thin bark that makes Nancy laugh — scampers up onto her blue Missoni sheets.

"Get down," says Nancy, as she reads Jody Jacob's society column in the *Los Angeles Times,* scanning the print for her name. Nothing. A pout flickers across her face. There has been nothing in *Vogue* (which she has piled up in a corner of the bedroom) for three years. And only a few mentions in *W, the* journal of fashion and New Celebrity.

Suddenly she feels like shopping and lunch at the Bistro.

That reminds her. She has to call Lucille Ball about a backgammon game. "I *love* Lucy," she says, not realizing her quip. "I mean, she loves me because she knows I was a figure-skating champion back in the sixties. I won the bronze at Squaw Valley, right? I've found her to be such a *real* person."

The telephone won't stop ringing. All her girlfriends are calling and she is getting the latest news and offering sweet, sympathetic whimpers to those who have suffered what can only be labeled the tragedies of the shopping set.

"Oh God," screams Nancy, "I'm so tired of women's liberation. It's so old. So passé. So gauche. It's boring. I mean, women who grab men and just pester them about how horrible they are, and *then* phone their girlfriends to talk about it, are ridiculous. That's two years ago. The right people enjoy *now*."

Twenty minutes later Nancy enters the Right Bank Clothing Company, considered, according to her, the newest fun boutique on Rodeo Drive in Beverly Hills. She is being treated like an old friend. (No wonder: Her then fiancé, multimillionaire apparel manufacturer Sam Bretzfield, was co-owner.)

"Hi, Lois," she greets Lois Pliner, the ex-wife of another owner of the store, who has dressed for the rainy day in a St. Tropez rain hat.

Then she spots *it*. "Oh, divine, divine ... precious, precious ... oh, my God, it's heavenly." It is a $500 gold-lamé raincoat, just in from Italy.

She rushes to it. "God, I'm like a gambler when I see something new I like," she says. (She resists the coat for exactly twenty-four hours, buying it the next day.) "I mean, I tell everybody I'm sick, then the whole world should be this sick. Shopping is so great, don't you know? It's a high. I mean, dope is stupid. I love to see all these people in society on dope and drunk at parties. That way I can really discover their inner personalities. But for me, grass is stupid. I fall asleep on it. I could fall asleep while I'm eating at the Bistro and my face could fall flat on the plate. I mean, right in the middle of the chocolate mousse."

She doesn't care, she says, that the arbiters of society consider her a "fringie" — a species that uses clothes, labels, symbols, furniture, names, anything to get into the big society columns.

"*Let* them close the doors on me," she explains, as she runs into the parking lot to fetch her two favorite coats — an $18,000 fox and a $17,000 mink — out of the unlocked trunk of her unlocked $65,000 Rolls-Royce Corniche. "I mean, the young people on their way up — people like me who are only thirty-three are fun people. Society the way you read about it — that serious dreary stuff in the *Times* — is a bunch of crap. But we have money. And dear, money may be awful. But it's really more awful if you haven't got it. I feel sorry for those old frumps. They'll fall. And we'll rise. I mean, it's going to be the rise of people with very good taste."

She's on Rodeo searching for some new objects again when she sees Candice Bergen, the actress. "Look at her," she says, like a fan. "She's been on the cover of *Town and Country,* you know. And she's sooooo beautiful. She's *somebody.*" Suddenly Nancy feels like shopping.

"Let's go to Bijan," she says, and she arrives at one of Rodeo's biggest showplaces with all the fanfare of visiting royalty. The owner, Bijan Pakzad, who spent $500,000 for a gilded staircase which Hollywood designers are comparing to a Cecil B. DeMille production, kisses her hand.

"I feel good," says Nancy. "Service is *not* gone. I've never wanted to be waited on — to make people feel like servants. Here they know how to make it work. They know it's crap. But they love it. Because it's illusion, glamour. It's being treated like a movie star. I love it."

She appraises several $800 suits and a $300 silk shirt. Then she discovers the gold-embossed plaque on a wall, which reels off the names of recent visitors to the shop, including Frank Sinatra, Senator Edward Kennedy, and football hero O. J. Simpson. "I'm so impressed," Nancy beams at the owner. Then she spots the name of King Hussan II of Morocco. "The king?" she asks, pushing up her big, round sunglasses (the kind Jackie O wears) for a better look. "I think the king can afford me. I'm sure the other men have lots of money, but the king would never run out." She turns back to Pakzad.

"You know, I wanted to copy your staircase for my new home on Bellagio in Bel Air. But I don't think I could do it as well."

"Oh, I'm on Bellagio too," crows Bijan's owner. "I'm right next door to Quinn Martin, the TV producer."

"Well," says Nancy, "I live next to Mrs. Alfred Hitchcock."

Friends live around Beverly Hills. "Sandra Bennett, *Mrs. Tony Bennett?*" Nancy asks at the Right Bank Tea Room for her usual salad. "Don't you think shopping is a higher consciousness thing right now?"

"I don't know," answers Mrs. Bennett, a Southern belle from upper Louisiana who feels that Nancy has potential as a person and as a new social leader in L.A. "I can't sit around and ponder things like that. What I want to know is, who owns the real estate around here? I hear Gloria Swanson's got a pile of it. I think Garbo too."

"Oh, they must have been wonderful human things," says Nancy. "Come on, let's go to Giorgio's."

"Isn't this fun?" Nancy is asking as she tries on an $800 peasant dress, screaming how it makes her look like a Tijuana waitress.

Then it's up to the shoe salon, searching for sandals and talking about shopping as a work of art. "You see, we shopping women here," says Nancy, "we serious women who know, who create taste — we have seen the Freddie Haymans, the Donald Pliners, the Herbie Finks of Theodore rise from nothing. People think it's dull to shop. It's not. It's fun. It's like going to the casinos in Vegas. You play for the high stakes. I love it. But I love watching the people as much as I love the shopping. The greatest games in the world are going on here. Much better than anything on TV.

"Everybody thinks that women like me are awful," she says as she parks her Rolls at the I. Magnin lot. "They put us down. But I don't go around putting anybody down. I don't harm anyone, do I? I'm a person, and I shop and I enjoy the great things of life. But I feel I'm okay, you're okay, you know what I mean?"

She wants to pursue these topics, so she suggests the Polo Lounge of the Beverly Hills Hotel at 5:30.

A man, someone she knew in Hollywood long before her social days when she was still getting write-ups like "the last of the Hollywood starlets" in *Cosmopolitan,* recognizes her and kisses her hand.

"Doing the Cosmo thing was fun," she says. "I was shot by Scavullo. I think Frank is one of the best *indoor* photographers, don't you? I think he's wonderful."

She is also terribly proud to be the first young member of the Amazing Blue Ribbon 400, a prestigious Los Angeles group — led by Mrs. Norman Chandler, mother of the *Times* publisher and grande dame of culture in Southern California — which supports the Music Center. "Buff," she says, whispering Mrs. Chandler's nickname.

"You know, *Dorothy* Chandler is *so* nice. She is so helpful, too. She told me at the very first meeting to say something. She said, 'You young people should speak up.' But I didn't know what to say. I couldn't understand a word they were saying. It didn't make a great deal of sense. But it's terribly important and good for the community."

Dinner is at Dominick's. "It's the greatest place," she says. "They only have three things on the menu, and you can't even get in unless the owner knows you are important. The right people all go there because they won't let anyone in that isn't tasteful or wants to sit around and be boring and talk about how terrible it is to shop and have fun."

About eleven she gets the *greatest* idea. "Hey, why don't we go to Acapulco?" she shouts, absolutely filled with joy at her grand idea. "I think we should go there and see the jet setters. They have some wonderful shops there. But most of all they have the greatest people. Wonderful people. People who are so rich that they pay people *not* to have their names put in society columns. That's real class."

In a minute, she is in the Rolls heading for the airport, but then she thinks better of it. "It's not the season," she pouts. "The best time is around Christmas."

She turns the car and it hits her — she feels like shopping. At this hour, only a coin-operated Laundromat is open. So she attacks her hair, fluffing and combing it. ("I couldn't let Beverly Hills hairdressers get their hands on it. I *only* have it done in New York. By the same man who does Margaux Hemingway's hair. Oh, she's a *good* friend of mine.")

"I take *Architectural Digest*. Don't you? All the good people do. I mean, where have you been living all your life? Orange County? Do people live out there? I was working a backgammon business. That's how it got so chic. I had so many damn backgammon games going that I had to scream and yell at my employees. They called me Dragon Lady. I said *enough*. I sympathize with people who have to work for a living. But that's not my ambition. I want to enjoy. I want life to be like an Elizabeth Taylor movie. I want to be free like she is, and say outrageous things. I like being a star. All the women who shop do. We're all in show biz in these stores. We are dressing a fantasy. I have no shame about it."

She has come to the dropping-off spot. "Well, goodie-bye," she says. "We'll go to Acapulco. You'll meet all the fun people. All the best. See you on Rodeo."

16 BOYS TOWN – THE WEEKEND

MONDAY

Paradise and Michael were back by the edge of the sea. It was at its most wondrous that morning. So quiet. Not like an ocean at all, more like a lake. A lake of blue velvet where white sailboats were placed like toys. You could not view the sea from Boys Town. The main cultural activity seemed to be sex. The only reason it had become a neighborhood at all was because it was so close to Hollywood and because men of a certain sexual preference needed their own territory.

Paradise and Michael had decided to break through the barriers of Boys Town. To flee from the lush prison yards of unreality and fantasy. The magic words were *I Love You.* Words almost unheard of in the vocabulary of Boys Town. Michael had explained his affair with Blackie Norton. Paradise had confessed his romance with Silver. They had both been offered the most important dream of the gay world — stardom. Silver had optioned Paradise for a three-movie deal. Blackie had promised Michael a featured role as a waiter at Ciro's West. Neither Michael nor Paradise, however, was buying.

They had returned to the sea the morning after Blackie's bacchanal because it had been their only touch of beauty during the weekend. Like two children they stared out at the horizon looking for kingdoms far different from Boys Town for their future together.

Then they departed. Paradise drove the van toward Northern California. The couple, arm in arm, watched the monumental estates and the towering haciendas vanish along the beachfront. Suddenly they were beyond the boundaries of Los Angeles. Green fields filled with wildflowers lined the sides of the road which rolled up and down the oceanfront.

Just before the tiny beach city of Oxnard, in a field of lettuce plants by the roadside, they spotted a hitchhiker. He had long blond hair. He wore a green backpack. Tall and straight. The hitchhiker carried a cardboard sign: BOYS TOWN.

No matter how far Michael and Paradise would go in the opposite direction, the world was headed toward Boys Town. If only out of curiosity to see a worldwide gay wonder.

Paradise stepped on the gas pedal. The van sped into the countryside. The hitchhiker waved. He did not know what lay ahead.

―――

Liberty noticed the wedding announcement in the morning *Times*: SPORTS HERO TO WED CHEERLEADER. It wouldn't be exactly a marriage. The town was starting to get the message that Liberty was bent. The marriage would also help Liberty negotiate a new million-dollar contract as a wedding present to himself and his bride.

There was a time for gayness and there was a time for straightness. As Liberty left Blackie Norton's that morning he realized that he wouldn't be returning to its Babylonian pleasures for quite some time.

Liberty was a balanced man. He had practically ruined his reputation. Now it was time to begin preserving what was left of his character.

At the corner of Santa Monica and LaBrea Boulevard in the section known as Fag Hollow, Liberty spotted a blond youth leaning against a telephone pole. His T-shirt bore the inscription HEAVEN. Just one last time, Liberty thought. One last time.

═══

Blackie Norton did not fool himself. He had no intention of ever leaving Boys Town. Not while there was an unsuspecting innocent to exploit arriving. Blackie had driven at top speed to Ciro's West that morning. When he arrived at his office he watched a private screening of the previous night's orgy. He found himself, through the magic of film, vicariously in bed with Liberty and Paradise. Paradise was going to be a major star. If he could make love to women on the screen the way he made love to men in private bedrooms, then romance would return to the screen.

Blackie Norton had only a few friends. Only one really. Himself. He had always made it a rule in Boys Town never to get close to another homosexual.

He counted the receipts from the weekend at Ciro's West. He didn't care if columnists had written that disco was kaput. His palace was grossing more than *Grease*.

Blackie lit up a Dunhill cigarette with a book of matches from Gucci. There was a call. A Mideastern oil sheik was in town and wanted to experience the erogenous zones of Boys Town.

Perfect. Blackie was looking for an excuse to throw an

other Sunday afternoon poolside party. Everyone would want to attend. Oil sheiks were as big as movie stars in Boys Town.

Blackie made a detailed list of every Hollywood star that the oil sheik desired to meet. Discovered exactly what his sexual needs would be. He spoke distinctly into the phone.

Certainly Blackie would take care of him. Didn't he always?

17 THE PARTY

ALLAN CARR'S HOLLYWOOD PARTY to end all parties begins each day at 10 A.M. By then, Carr will have risen from his opulent bed, trotted energetically to his opulent bath, and thrown wide the doors to a world that few will ever experience.

Carr is a movie producer (*Grease, Can't Stop the Music*), and a former super-agent (Ann-Margret, Stockard Channing, Tony Curtis, Dyan Cannon) who shocked supposedly unshockable Hollywood in the sixties when he arrived in town from Chicago, bought Ingrid Bergman's old hideaway in Benedict Canyon, and began showing up at such staid, conservative hangouts as Chasen's Restaurant wearing a full-length Blackglama mink coat and white, soiled tennis shoes. That was a bit too much, even for turned-on Hollywood. Not only that, Carr opened his mini-mansion (really much too small for a man of his legend, everyone said) to bacchanals of such a wide assortment of tastes that people referred to his estate, the tree-laden forest outside his Tudor chalet with the incredibly large, turquoise swimming pool statused-up with some French baroqueries, as Mount Olympus.

There are two things you never discuss in Hollywood. One is drugs. The other is homosexuality. That might explain the presence of straight stars, socialites, and business types in Carr's place at night. By day the crowd was gay. The rule of order in the town was that anyone stepping foot in Carr's place fell into one of three categories: brains, money, or ass. Even now gorgeous boys — tanned, bronzed, fine-toned, golden, Wasp, blond, blue-eyed, straight-teethed — were descending the magnificently carpeted stairways from the netherworld of Carr's upstairs bedrooms and floating majestically toward the pool. From his bedroom, Carr would watch them in popsicle-colored Speedo swimsuits marching in unison toward the chaise longues by the pool, draped in terry-cloth towels. Carr had given such wonders of the world a name: Twinkies. Later, when everyone in tout Hollywood picked up on the term for the golden ones who came to Cinema City searching for fame and fortune, Carr changed the name to Triscuits. Whatever you called them, the town regarded such goings-on as equal to the end of Western Civilization. Roman, they called it. Like some emperor in a Biblical epic, they said. And Hollywood loved every minute of it. They had come from Florida, Nebraska, Ohio, South Dakota, Wisconsin for *this*. The overstatement. The extravagance. The unequaled decadence. There was nothing like it. Not anywhere. Europe had fallen under the Black Plague of Socialism. Upper-class Europeans no longer had entrée to flaunt their opulent lifestyles. London was a mess. New York too provincial and conservative. Only Hollywood could produce a modern wonder like Carr. The last of the Grands Seigneurs. A man who bubbled like champagne and was now sitting in his Sheik Chic Arabian cabana — stocked with overstuffed caramel-colored Valentino pillows — watching every fantasy imaginable appear before his eyes. A living testament to the fact that pizzazz had not vanished from the face of Hollywood.

Today Carr is wearing a Theodore sport shirt, a pair of faded Calvin Klein jeans, and Gucci loafers without socks. His dark hair is cut in a youthful, trendy style. His massive frame stretched out in the shadows of the cabana. Twenty-one phone extensions are at his elbow, connecting him instantly with every section of his ivy-covered chateau — a vision from a Great Castles of the Century manual — always stocked with ten to fifteen friends and assorted Twinkies.

Already crispy rolled, thin, $140-an-ounce joints are being passed among the glitterati by the pool. Dynamite weed. Everyone is starved to perfection, even the older queens, who come to gawk at the majesty of the Carr empire and the younger men in their sleek swimsuits stretched out on the richly colored couches and covered head to toe with gold jewelry. *Only* 14 karat, but symbols of the fact that they had been bought and sold and finally ended up at the greatest party in Hollywood. Youth was the key. Coffee, finely ground Jurgensen's mocha roast, is served by smiling servants. Someone brings croissants. Cartier watches gleam in the sunlight. Gold chains from Tiffany and Gucci boggle the senses. The lawn is manicured.

Two hundred people — all major in some way, all regularly featured in the pages of *Town and Country* — are housed in hotels around the city awaiting the dark and their entrance to Carr's continuous roadshow party. The hottest people in the world had always wanted to break loose in Hollywood.

Those who knew — the right people — flocked to Carr's as they would to a trashy novel in which all the names were named. It was hot in California, and the life was loose. There were hardly any intellectuals. And no governments imposing restrictions. So suddenly Hollywood had become fascinating again. All those palm trees or something. The last outpost of extravaganza. Everything that anyone could possibly overdo was being overdone in triplicate: overdrinking, oversexing, overdrugging, overspending, and overindulging in life as a pleasure. Endless pleasure.

Who remembers when we all fell in love with the Hollywood Dream? It was so American. Fame. Fortune. Stardom. Glamour. Riches. Tits and Ass. And now, boys. It was as if the searchlights shooting through the city's sky were guiding Western Civilization back to Rome. Most homes of the Hollywood nobles had Roman terraces and sparkling swimming pools, and the population drove the most beautiful chariots. Every day it was down to shop in Beverly Hills. Off to the spa. Tennis. Jogging. Every night the pleasure of the great baths like Carr's. There you could experience any fantasy. A Hollywood gay. Being with a beautiful, horny Italian actor. Being with the most beautiful and available girls. Doing exotic drugs. Meeting someone casually and having an insanely wild affair. Talking to the counts and countesses of Europe. The company of the most sought-after Hollywood stars. You could fuck Mr. Universe. You could fuck your best friend's husband before his unconscious wife. Most were young, or younger than Carr, who admitted to thirty-nine, and they all were capable of causing outrageous scenes.

Brains. Money. Ass. Allan Carr couldn't have made it this far into the show-biz history books without the first two. And the asses were available at his beck and call. His wealth was understood. After all, darling, he had reportedly received a check from Paramount for the first six months' revenues off *Grease* for $13 million. Carr had marketed *The Deer Hunter*, a picture Universal wanted to throw out to the drive-ins in Iowa, into an Oscar winner and a box-office blockbuster. If Carr could do that with Vietnam, think what he could do with something, well, salable.

Carr had his own reasons for creating a set for himself and a court life that constituted the last hit of Babylon for Hollywood. The portly, gay, not-so-golden boy from upper-crust Chicago (his real name, Alan Solomon) had bought himself love and security. His illnesses were talked about. The intestinal bypass operation. The kidney stone trip. His weight problems were legend. Having his mouth wired to avoid his sumptuous all-hours banquets. Going to Duke University for the rice diet. But, despite the fact that some of his enemies thought Carr resembled Divine playing Auntie Mame, and his chutzpah, loud voice, and incredible grand vision of the gay sensibility had shocked the heterosexual straight society of Hollywood, he would come to stand as a symbol of Hollywood in the eighties. Carr was kind, for one thing. He was incredibly generous, for another. He seemed to understand that what California was exporting was the idea of the endless party. Many figured he invented High Hollywood. It was not unusual for Carr to mastermind a celebrity safari of 200 to a rock concert and provide each guest with a bag of snorts, three joints, and a bottle of the best champagne from the Wine Merchant in Beverly Hills. There was nothing Hollywood liked better than taking someone so "out" and making him "in." So society looked the other way at the golden-boy Twinkies, and waited in the bushes of Carr's gardens in the moonlight to find themselves drawn toward boy worship as if the world had gone crazy with oral fixation.

Carr had his masculine side. He was a ball breaker in making deals. A master of the fifteen-second phone transaction. But even Carr realized that the only deals worth mentioning in Hollywood were taking place upstairs at his mansionette. There Hollywood got down. Days of wild and frenzied overindulgence finally mellowed into a space where fantastic sums of super-money passed hands the way that guests passed a golden-stemmed glass of champagne. The limousines to the studios the day after the party were only sweat-soaked public displays of gentlemen's agreements made the night before. On such royal occasions Carr had to display the persona of a Renaissance Pope. All of El Lay aware of his movings and comings. They had seen the stories in *People* and *New West*. The two-page Norman Sieff photograph in blazing Technicolor filling up *Life*. The endless television chat-show appearances. But Hollywood knew the rules. Carr was in an echelon far beyond shopping at Safeway, wandering down Rodeo, or cruising Santa Monica Boulevard. He had spread his magic dust of fantasy on Hollywood — and only a few were privileged enough to get the proper hit.

Carr's gargantuan musings now centered around the life at the pool. Aimlessly, two golden boys discussed a recent trek to Palm Springs and their encounters with Hollywood gossip columnist Rona Barrett. God, they told each other in voices of television commercial princes, Rona was such a supporter of gay liberation. Not that there was anything wrong with that. All the Hollywood women were adopting gay boys as part of the latest luxury of legendary fame. But Miss Rona was sooo tacky. Jesus, that Corvette styrofoam hair in pink curlers was just too much. And a woman of her age should never appear in public in a black and white bikini.

Then it was a time for a Quaalude, a drug which the Twinkies served around the pool because it relaxed them for the ultra-tan. Thoughts of Miss Rona vanished from their awareness. After all, Miss Rona was just another legend.

About 2 P.M., when the first or second 'lude of the day wore off, everyone — ten to fifteen hangers-on — the Twinkies, the staff, would move inside the cool, dusty interiors of the mansionette for lunch. After changing into casual sports clothes, they sat down to an incredibly large lunch of a tossed green salad with everything tossed on it one can imagine, hot french bread, served in long pioneer loaves, tuna molds garnished with lemon wedges, roast chicken, potato salad, in another mold, garnished with parsley and tomatoes. The wine was good. The servants stacked all the glass plates, the silverware, and the napkins from Pottery Barn and Geary's North on a circular glass table. The stemmed wine goblets were large. Many of the guests arrived from bedrooms nearby. It is a scene that most people never witness. A painting of a society filled with great fanfare. The guests drove Jaguars and Sevilles and Mercedeses. You were only as pretty as you felt. And these people felt pretty. An eight-foot plaster of Paris replica of an Oscar stood at the doorway of the house. Soft breezes from the ocean caressed the sun-soaked bodies. The bathrooms in the mansionette had wallpaper copied from such legendary watering holes of Hollywood as the old Mocambo and Ciro's nightclubs. Allan Carr's bed had once belonged to the magnificent, billboard-sized body of fifties starlet Kim Novak. Mink coats were used as bedcovers. The talk was full of manners and not much mores. No one cared what was happening on the six o'clock news. It was all too negative, anyway. Carr's guests preferred the prefab chatter in *WWD*.

Gay sources estimated the homosexual population of Hollywood to be as high as 75 percent. When Allan Carr arrived at the golden gates of Hollywood studios in the early sixties the gay sensibility was not a popular subject of discussion. Famous people had homosexual affairs, of course, but didn't discuss them. Now, however, fading Hollywood actors accompanied by their younger lovers appeared on the guest lists of even the chicest parties. The smart people knew that a few unattached men must be invited to any respectable party. Any unattached man who showed — no matter how great a star — was openly admitting he would be available sexually to the most beautiful man or woman at the party. The gay sensibility had formed around Hollywood. It was open — and thriving. And providing Hollywood with fresh cocktail conversation.

There was even a Hollywood Gay Mafia, a whole marketplace that employed only gays. Certainly everyone gave gays credit for introducing butyl nitrate or poppers into Hollywood high society. The boys were back in town. Landing at all entrances of Hollywood to become waiters, bartenders — until they met somebody willing to make them a houseboy. All the golden boys seemed to be getting their portfolios together, looking for modeling jobs. But most of them had some physical imperfection. They were too nellie. Had bad hair. Or bad teeth. The only ones allowed through the doors of Hilhaven were 100 percent perfect.

At nightfall Carr left the cabana — where he ruled over his kingdom like a modern potentate — passed the swimming pool and pressed switches to light up his estate. Blue lights. Walt Disney cartoon colors. Red lights around the pool. Glittering, Tinkerbell Christmas lights around the bars.

Candles were lighted at all entrances, in all rooms by a procession of servants who moved past the medieval-like windows like monks. Hilhaven was transformed into a rich amusement park. If you were getting an aerial view, flying in on a helicopter, you would have suspected you were dropping in on a festival. In the world of the jet set, around Régine's or Studio 54, they would remember the lights going on at Allan Carr's.

Here was glamour. The most beautiful women in the world arriving after dinners at Le Dome or Morton's and looking absolutely gorgeous. Glorious men dressing down or dressing up. Allan Carr at the door in a bejeweled caftan greeting guests. An abundance of highs. A great deal of champagne, Carr's favorite beverage. Everyone said the same thing on entering the scene — climbing into the mood as if preparing for a lavish roller-coaster ride — if you didn't have anyone turning you onto real-life adventure, this would be the place. Jesus, no one overentertains like a movie producer pope.

Carr had also transformed. The signs of business worries had vanished from his brow. At all entrances and exits he emerged, a drink in hand, a wittily prepared remark for everyone. Allan Carr knew how to make a party hot.

Close your eyes. Think of yourself inside a tunnel, then coming out into the light and a scene resembling Paradise. Forests of trees lit in the manner of Disneyland. Rock-and-roll music — or whatever is happening at that moment in New York dance halls and wouldn't reach California for at least six months — is pouring from loudspeakers. Scores of beautiful people are climbing red-carpeted steps to the pace of the music. The smell of rich perfume trailing blonde, Wasp, thoroughbred women dressed in tight-fitting Fiorucci Spandex jeans and see-through tops. Or dark-haired beauties in Yves Saint Laurent, with dresses of black Lurex-trim fabric, mostly concealed by enormous, long, black scarves wrapped around their entire bodies. All flashing beautiful Palm Springs tans. Or watch the Europeans on vacation, with their hidden vials in their pockets. Someone — a bald-headed man in a violet-colored cotton shirt, collarless, and a puritanical look of contempt on his face — is going around telling everybody not to get high, that Hollywood is the downfall of Western Civilization. But blondie, the one with the rotating rear which is now rubbing against an agent's hand, blows a blast from a thin cigarette in his general direction.

Jackie Bisset has arrived. The women in the room glance in her direction, giving the first movie star of the night the once-over. Good hair, bone structure, teeth, tits, ass, nice expression. They recognize the look. They've all attended the same acting classes. The studio training. They've all gone down to publicity to get the gowns to wear to the premières. But this scene is different. This is not the *Valley of the Dolls*. This is *Future Shock*. Bisset smiles, awaiting the flashbulbs from the cameramen who might earn $150 from the news services for pictures of her. Bisset, like the other stars arriving — there's Polly Bergen over by the stairs talking to Barbara Rush, and Olivia Newton-John in a pair of shorts and a Peter Pan–collared shirt — always acted totally respectable.

It was bullshit, Jacqueline Bisset would agree. But the bullshit of Hollywood was back after having been placed in suspended animation during the hippie era. God, the only action a young actress could find in the scripts of the sixties was acting like a zombie on acid and waiting for a long-haired, thin, emasculated superstar with acne to mount her while the screen flashed colored lights. These days, the old glamour bullshit had returned. After all, the image of the star is what made Hollywood great. Caused all those young men in Kansas or wherever to dream dreams at night. Women were back, groomed for stardom in every possible way. Suddenly women attempted to walk with poise again, and behave with propriety. Bisset gazed at the soap opera in front of her and didn't mind becoming a leading character. Afterward, at home, she could be just Jacqueline Bisset. Bisset was lucky. She could talk. Could contribute something beyond idle chitchat about the latest fashions. At Carr's you didn't need to be articulate. Just to float.

Dean-Paul Martin, Dean Martin's son, had entered. His face could have been improved. He didn't have a full mouth, had a sharp nose and a severely angular chin. Yet he was still by far the most beautiful man in the room.

One woman, who described herself as a magazine editor, was creating pandemonium among the women because she had dyed the ends of her Italian couture haircut purple. She had it done, announced a pencil-thin woman in a voice of the purest aristocratic bent, at Vidal Sassoon's and it was called Flying Colors. Purple, well, that was understood to be *the* royal color this year. Her daddy had told her she was nothing but a royal bitch and only her daddy could get away with something like that. She then trailed off into the voices and the music to seek a new audience.

She was replaced by a wild-eyed blonde, about thirty-one, with two gold stars placed in her unruly hair and wearing a Brioni shirt and two skirts resembling a maid's uniform. The costume had been featured last month in *Italian Vogue*. This woman was incredibly high. 'Ludes, coke, liquor — she grabbed at any escape mechanism that High Hollywood offered. She was searching, she said, for one straight man. Just one straight man — maybe a chipmunk, a little five-foot-six type like Buck Henry. She was suffering from a wretched case of acid indigestion and began burping up the most stupefying gurgles of gazpacho imaginable. Accompanying this blonde (natural, my dear), who was attempting to outdo Ava Gardner on her most tempestuous nights and was screaming at passers-by that she must release her nervous energy, that she was out to cause trouble, was a younger man of enormous physique and prince-like blonde hair claiming to be a fluff boy for *Playgirl*.

A good portion of the guest list came supplied with their own highs. However, Allan Carr *was* the perfect host. And a boy, designated to supply the visitors, roamed freely through the crowd. The guests wanted action. They were into a central rush — 400 of the very best together in one gigantic snake of sensuality. In Hollywood they know how to stroke, baby. Who cared about the "A" parties? Those society snobs thought that a real fun evening was getting screwed three times in the sauna.

Cher's voice pulsated from the sound system. Pure Dolby. Sensurround. Music seemed to be emanating from the heavens, the hells, the rivers, the valleys. Guests didn't care by this time about their stardom. Things were loose.

This was the Oscar they wanted for the night. They might have lost the Academy Award, but tonight they were winning. They had made it up to the heights. More was to come. Much more.

Downstairs at Hilhaven was even more Night Lifey in Carr's King Tut dance hall. Here it was. Past the *Grease* posters, past the portraits of Ann-Margret, past the Bella Darvi bar — golden and royally decadent — a noise rushed through the adrenalin systems of Hollywood. At one time it had been status in the town to hold private screenings. Carr had changed all that. At considerable expense, some estimated over $1 million, he had designed the first at-home disco in a former rumpus room. Pure Arabian Nights.

Fantasia. Guests took one look at the mock-Egyptian male statues with skimpy loincloths around their private goodies and the 18-karat-gold DJ booth and freaked. Those who couldn't get it up to dance lay back against the richly upholstered banquettes and sipped champagne.

Sparkling lights like a theater marquee blasted the senses. Sweaty, steamy dancers of all sexual persuasions gyrated before their eyes. Hollywood was hardly dead. In fact, it was beginning all over again.

The press was not allowed upstairs. The press, like George Christy, a regular who wrote about parties in his column, "The Great Life," in the *Hollywood Reporter,* were aware of the Olympian heights. But Hollywood journalists remained downstairs, maintaining a respectable distance from the overindulgence of appetites in the thickly carpeted rooms above.

For guests, the earlier you arrived at Hilhaven, the better. For you had your pick of the rooms. All, that is, except the master bedroom, which was reserved for Carr's phone calls. Allan Carr didn't need to read the trade papers; he received the latest news of the entertainment world piped into his home each night. Was Goldie Hawn pregnant? Carr would be the first to know. Was Hollywood's latest $30-million epic in trouble? Carr made it his business to find out. At 2, 3, 4, 5, 6, 7, 8 A.M. the calls would come. And Carr raced to the Princess phone, grabbed the receiver with his own hands, heavily laden with Bulgari jewelry, spread his frame, covered with the richest designs of the fashion slaves who courted his wealth and power on his bed, and gave his best performances. Carr would cajole, he would purr, and he would get to the bottom line of any Hollywood tragedy, marital dispute, or deal within thirty seconds. His enemies labeled him a monster, the most powerful manipulator of the American Dream since Darryl F. Zanuck. Yet in Hollywood enemies soon turned to friends. After all, this was Hollywood.

One room was locked. Prowling guests soon moved to the next door to find a bedroom decorated like a luxurious stateroom on an Italian steamliner, with nothing out of place except a few tattered Vuitton suitcases thrown in a corner. The couple inside on the bed had left the door ajar. Why not, they had evidently decided, let anyone who wanted discover exactly what it was like to make love in Hollywood in the eighties? The man resembles an Italian aristocrat but is actually a screenwriter. The woman is an ex–pro football cheerleader turned actress. Her breasts are large and firm enough to qualify as cultural stereotypes.

When it was over — and every participant had blasted the night with his own particular brand of sexual reverie — they all laughed. Then they vanished. one by one, into the night. Back to the party to portray their public personas. And to do this all over again.

As in a Hollywood movie the attention of the guests switched from the moonlit sexual rites, past the red-lit swimming pool, past the diners feasting at the white tables on the manicured lawns, to center on a white-shuttered window in the mansionette. Inside the guest room, referred to as the Destruction Derby Room, a charming studio decorated with country fixtures, two women were discussing the finer points of Hollywood divorce. After all, what was a Hollywood party without the standard fight scene? The women, both in their forties, were well beyond being great ass. Still they were both great beauties and possessors between them of at least $2 million in property rights.

One of the women, Dagny, whose main preoccupation in real life was organizing groups of women and weekly treks to trashy movies — and who knew Governor Jerry Brown quite well — was upset. She had just caught her husband making it with a starlet. "That bastard," she said in a voice part Bette Davis, part Joan Crawford. "We'll let him chase after that nineteen-year-old cunt. I hope she slashes him. I hope she tears off his balls. I was nineteen once and I was pretty too. They all wanted me. God, why did they make me a Catholic?"

The other woman, whose name appeared frequently in society columns and who had made it to the top in Hollywood via marriage to a studio executive, listened politely as she smoked a low-tar cigarette. She had heard such stories of Hollywood infidelities many times before. But she appreciated Dagny's performance. This woman confiding in her was astute enough about the games in Hollywood to win an Oscar.

Dagny had fine, black hair which she pulled back from her forehead in a style known in chic circles as the status pull. She was shaking in full melodramatic fury. She had married this guy, she said, right out of school. Had his baby. Thrown his goddamn parties. Now he was chasing after Dolly Parton–like starlets and calling Switzerland on deals.

Like a general Dagny planned her divorce strategy. She would throw Danny out, she told the other woman, who placed her cigarette in a crystal ashtray and appeared slightly interested. Then suddenly Dagny became very interesting. She pulled some smuggled cocaine cut with heroin from her Gucci bag. Have a toot, she offered.

They talked for a long time, the coke producing a high

which made them feel omnipotent. The woman leaned back into her armchair and shook her hair. She was now going to hear the great Hollywood soap opera. The divorce story. Dagny lay back on the bed and pressed her hand along the borders of her Charles Gallay silk skirt. It hadn't been bad. Living in Hollywood, she said. At first it had been glorious. All the lushness. Nothing like staid Boston. They had climbed. Bought the goddamn right furniture. The shitty little "A" circle–approved florists. Threw the crummy press parties. Let the world picture them as a golden couple. Always shimmering with enough style to attract the best people. Still, was this a life? Hell, she didn't even have someone who would come to her rescue if she placed a dime in a pay telephone.

The other woman never spoke. Merely listened. This woman had been to the best shrinks in the world. They were all in Beverly Hills listening at three in the morning to women like Dagny telling the truth about the great life. There were more psychiatrists in Hollywood than there were stars. So, as a long-time resident, the woman knew how to "psych out" better than how to prepare a spectacular meal. Underneath all the static, the woman felt that Dagny was very brave. Like a wonderful horse. And she perceived that Dagny was talented. Of course, she had never *done* anything, just lived a rich, fantasy life. Yet she could have. As she inspected Dagny she made mental notes. Too fat. The body would have to be whipped into shape at a spa — maybe the Golden Door. But a dazzling personality. After careful consideration, she felt that she could definitely get Dagny back into the marketplace. Wasn't that what Dagny was really talking about? Getting a man. That was paramount in Hollywood. If you didn't have a man and were over forty nothing happened in your life.

She knew Dagny's husband. Nice man. Good, straight stuff. But dull. Dagny could do better. Reaching over she brushed a tear from Dagny's eye. Not the touch of a lesbian. The touch of a woman who compassionately understood how downs could take one off the Allan Carr trip. You could survive in Hollywood only if you were up. Any signs of weakness beneath the armor cost points off your status in town. That was the game. You had to sparkle. Must be gods and goddesses free of the tragedies of the rest of the species.

She shot Dagny a look that a manager might give a burned-out prizefighter before he entered the ring. A look that caused Dagny to stand erect, brush her dress, and once again become the charming Miss Junior League who had made it in Hollywood. She might not be able to bed a rock star, but she was aware of the fact that men of her generation still appreciated a classy lady.

Dagny declared a new Bill of Rights. Also, she was ready to be fucked. Years disappeared from her life. Generations fell away. Pressures collapsed. She still had the instincts of her breed. Downstairs she rushed to Allan Carr to give him a hug. Then she marched over to the nearest man. She was charming and seductive and soon began to relish her new status as an available wife. It was so Hollywood, Dagny thought to herself, as a very attractive television producer gave her the eye. No matter how you tried the only thing that people would believe was the happy ending. It was either that or suicide. When she caught the eye of her husband, she gave him her best Audrey Hepburn–imitation smile. So what if he was chasing the young stuff? He could certainly afford it. Besides, the Twinkies would soon be closing in on fresh, available rich bait like *Jaws*.

It happened every night this way. As long as you were beautiful or had money. Legendary. Allan Carr was not a fantastic-looking man. Not by conventional standards. Nevertheless, he bubbled, and he was enthusiastic. And he believed in Hollywood. Each day he produced a movie epic from his life and cast it with the best talent available at the moment. He had decided to revive and refurbish the lost dream of Hollywood as the mecca of naughtiness and glamour. It would have been nice if Liza had been there sitting atop the piano to sing a Marvin Hamlisch tune. But, another night. Sooner or later all of Hollywood would arrive at Carr's. One by one.

Allan Carr delighted in spectacles. Now, it was time to disappear into the business world of the Master Bedroom.